LETTERS
TO
LÉONTINE ZANTA

PIERRE TEILHARD DE CHARDIN

LETTERS
TO
LÉONTINE ZANTA

INTRODUCTION BY
ROBERT GARRIC AND HENRI DE LUBAC

Translated by
BERNARD WALL

COLLINS
ST JAMES'S PLACE, LONDON
1969

Lettres à Léontine Zanta
was first published in 1965 by
Desclée de Brouwer

Nihil obstat John M. T. Barton STD, LSS Censor
Imprimatur Patrick Casey Vic. General
Westminster, 19th June 1968

The Nihil obstat and Imprimatur
are a declaration that a book or pamphlet is
considered to be free from doctrinal or moral error.
It is not implied that those who have granted
the Nihil obstat and Imprimatur agree
with the contents, opinions or
statements expressed.

Contents

·

Contents

Père Teilhard and Mademoiselle Zanta

BY ROBERT GARRIC

'So come and have lunch on Wednesday. You'll meet three priests who will not fail to interest you.'

It was on this invitation from Mademoiselle Zanta that I set out for Neuilly on a fine Spring day in 1925—my curiosity somewhat aroused. I had no idea of the deep significance the meeting would have for me.

Three priests were duly there. One was the famous Abbé Bremond. The second was also well known, Abbé Mugnier. The third was my surprise of the day. . . .

Abbé Bremond was no disappointment for anyone reasonably familiar with his books: his *Literary History of Religious Thought in France* had started coming out, revealing to French readers innumerable hitherto unknown mystics whom he expounded in his beautiful, poetic style. Abbé Bremond was thin and immensely tall; he looked down on you with lively mischievous eyes; subtle, sparkling remarks fell from his thin, tight lips, and he led the conversation. When I recalled how people had begun referring to him as a new Sainte-Beuve, I couldn't help feeling rather intimidated.

Abbé Mugnier seemed by contrast tiny, full of good nature and with a mischievous twinkle in his eye. His sparkling wit and the playful good-nature of his conversation were fascinating. His legend followed him: he had been Huysmans' confidant and had introduced him to the cathedral,[1] and was the friend and spiritual director

---

[1] J. K. Huysmans, the well-known decadent writer who was converted to Catholicism. *La Cathédrale* is his book about Chartres (Tr.).

of many artists and poets. Though made to listen, and to lift up suffering souls, he was love for poetry and the arts incarnate. He liked the romantics, held Combourg[1] and its master in reverence, and his eyes misted with whimsical emotion if one talked to him about his close literary friends or some book he appreciated. He had just discovered Marie Noël and proclaimed her a great poet; Abbé Bremond, too, was urging and encouraging her to persevere in her vocation.

The third priest stood out from the rest of the company. He was tall too, and slim, but spoke little; his fine deep-set eyes had a far-away look and seemed to be following some private train of thought. He joined in the conversation with much reserve, but what he said was weighty and incisive. He had dash and restraint. And both his silence and his quick interjections made an impression. You felt you were in the presence of someone with a powerful personality, and for whom you immediately felt enormous warmth. He had the lofty bearing of a gentleman in religious orders, and the lively gait of a champion runner. His face was lit with an inner life and lined by asceticism.

That day I marked him out for ever and said so to our hostess at whose home I was to meet him again later on. He was Père Teilhard de Chardin, just back from his first journey to China.

What was this friendly place where so many artists and philosophers gathered? And who was its mistress?

Mademoiselle Zanta's name and work were already well known. During the last ten years or so she had shown herself to have one of the most distinguished

---

[1] Medieval castle in Brittany where Chateaubriand spent part of his boyhood.

minds of her time, and her dazzling career had brought
her a number of admirers.

As a young Alsatian girl, the daughter of a teacher in
humanities, she had forced her parents to let her study
philosophy, sit for her baccalauréat at a time when girls
rarely sat for it, and move to Paris so as to attend courses
at the Sorbonne.

Before preparing for her licence she stayed in Egypt, in
Ismailia, with the family of a Monsieur Le Masson, chief
engineer for the Suez Canal, and was responsible for a
few months for the education of his three children. On
her return to Paris she taught and did coaching work,
helping her father with his pupils while reading for her
own examinations. She was the only woman philosophy
student in the Faculty. She fell under the spell of her beloved philosophers, Plato filled her with admiration, and
she developed a secret liking for Epictetus' 'Manual'—at
one time she almost knew it by heart. She attended the
lectures of Brochard, Émile Boutroux and Gabriel
Séailles. Then she got to know that superb master, Henri
Bergson, who was to have a deep influence over her ideas.

In 1898 she passed her licence in philosophy with flying
colours and threw herself enthusiastically into teaching—
her natural vocation. Vivid, sprightly, persuasive, speaking with warmth and precision, she never lost her appeal
to student audiences of both sexes. She taught at the Mutualité Maintenon, an institute of higher studies recently
created by Madame Paris, and in practice a non-State
teachers' training college. There she met Samuel Roche-
blave who became a lifelong friend, Paul Doumer, then
Governor-General of Indo-China, and honorary president of the establishment, and the historian and critic,
Alfred Mézières.

But with all this activity she never forgot her real and
lasting vocation. She was encouraged by Bergson, Séailles

and Strowski to take for her thesis in philosophy a subject then little explored, 'The Revival of Stoicism in
the Sixteenth Century.' When she was not teaching or
tutoring her many pupils, she spent her time in the Bib-
liothèque Nationale, and she also stole hours from the
night to write her first major work. Those around her
admired her cheerful persistence and her rare talent for
overcoming obstacles as if they were mere trifles. When
she became a Doctor of Philosophy on May 19, 1914, it
was a red-letter day for French feminism, for she was the
first Frenchwoman to face the ordeal.

That year also brought the war, and as an Alsatian
Mademoiselle Zanta followed its progress with intense
emotion. During those years she taught philosophy at
the lycée Buffon for boys, and was elected President of
the Mutualité Maintenon. Her influence quickly spread.
Almost against her will she came to play a leading part
in the French feminist movement.

Increasingly in demand to speak at a succession of con-
ferences and congresses, she soon became quite famous.
She did not share the violent passions about politics and
political rights expressed by some of her women colleagues in the literary and journalistic world: her main
concern was that women should have the right to take
up professional careers. It was during those years of in-
tensive work and early renown that she wrote her *Psychologie du féminisme*, to which Paul Bourget contributed
the preface. This brought her new friends and colla-
borators—among them Colette Yver.

By now she was defending women's professional rights
in the daily Press, and before long became a regular jour-
nalist of great ability with leading articles in the main
newspapers. Soon she widened her field of interest, and
tackled all sorts of educational and social problems. Her
method was to expound the situation, give her own point

of view, and then make a warm appeal for the cause she upheld. She tackled such questions as women factory-workers and non-State schools. Her distress over the divisions in her country caused her to write one day, with heartfelt stoicism: 'I am sitting at my desk trying to brace myself against the misfortunes of the times by re-reading the noble and melancholy thoughts of Marcus Aurelius.'

From now on her correspondence became enormous. Readers wrote to her with their thoughts and their problems, and this went on till the end of her life. She became involved in a vital dialogue with her country.

With her increasing fame also as a lecturer, Mademoiselle Zanta received invitations from abroad. The first foreign country she visited was Holland. In 1919 we find her in Rotterdam, speaking alternately in the large drawing-room of the woman-president of the *Alliance française*, and in the Notaries' Hall. There she embarked on her great theme: modern woman and the social problems of the twentieth century. Next she went to Belgium and her own beloved provinces of eastern France, where she was delighted to return. Her gifts came out best in debate, argument produced her liveliest answers, and she could always win confidence and a warm response from a roomful of listeners.

Socially she was much sought after. She was invited out and received many guests in her home. But though she shone in Paris gatherings, she loved getting back to the haven of the Avenue de Madrid in Neuilly where she and her family had been established since 1900. The atmosphere there suited her; she had furnished her study—frequented by so many illustrious guests—in an agreeable and harmonious style. Portraits of Erasmus and Justus Lipsius presided over those humanist conversations, and above the low bookcase was a reproduction of Raphael's Dispute of the Blessed Sacrament. Near the door stood

Michelangelo's Moses, and not far away was Pascal's death-mask.

And from her balcony, where she loved to linger in the evenings, and whence she could see the foliage of the Bois de Boulogne, she watched the 'lovely red or golden sun descending' below the horizon.

Though her home was made for wisdom and meditation, it was often invaded by the merry family of her nephew and niece and their children who lived in the neighbouring flat. It was also constantly visited by the friends whom Mademoiselle Zanta had gathered around her at an early stage and retained till the end of her life: Madame Darcanne, the distinguished doctor and one of the first woman house-surgeons in France; Marguerite Teillard-Chambon who had been one of her students and who had become a close friend (it was through her that she first met Père Teilhard de Chardin); the Comtesse Melchior de Polignac; Madame Le Masson with whom she had stayed in Ismailia.

It was a home where philosophers loved to meet and was already redolent with memories; for it was there (as Maurice Donnay has recounted) that Henri Bergson first met Père Sertillanges, at luncheon during the first world war. This first encounter, at which the Abbé Mugnier and Maurice Donnay were also present, led to others.

It was a home frequented not only by philosophers but by writers too: novelists, poets, travellers. The Tharaud brothers were constant visitors, as well as René Boylesve, Paul Bourget and Maurice Barrès—a neighbour. As Mademoiselle Zanta was a member of the jury for the Prix Fémina, young writers also attended her salon. I remember an evening when Joseph Kessel turned up; his vivacity and enthusiasm was matched only by her own.

By 1925 she was over fifty: her beauty was still outstanding and had gained, with age, an air of greater seriousness and serenity. The grace of her carriage and the charm of her expression—which defied the portrait-painter—suggested comparison with a Renaissance princess. She was the heroine of one of Colette Yver's novels —'that woman with snow-white hair, luminous features, a full round face, whose tender, merry, forget-me-not blue eyes were a constant and tempestuous reflection of her soul. . . .' As I remember her, Mademoiselle Zanta combined harmony and grace of movement with an expression of tender serenity and gently-burning fervour.

'The lamp', her pupils called her; 'Mademoiselle Lanéo' was Maurice Donnay's nickname; 'Hypatia' murmured the Abbé Bremond; and Madame Darcanne called her 'Our dear Zanta'. . . .

Mademoiselle Zanta kept Père Teilhard abreast of all her multiple activities. He followed her doings and encouraged her with his interest and friendship, and on each of his visits to Paris they tried to catch up with each other's news and ideas.

In 1925 Mademoiselle Zanta developed a further activity: she began giving a series of philosophical talks each year, bearing upon an important topic—'Lenten lectures' they were called—to a large audience of women desirous of improving their knowledge and their souls. Until 1929 these lectures took place at the *Revue des Jeunes*, and thereafter at her flat in the Avenue de Madrid. The subjects dealt with show where her interests lay: in 1925, The Problem of Free Will; in 1926, The Problem of Belief; in 1932, the Religious Problem of Blondel.

Sometimes she invited some other philosopher or writer to address her audience. Thus Daniel-Rops gave a talk in the Avenue de Madrid: Henri Gouhier did so too, soon after finishing his great thesis on Malebranche;

and no one will forget Jean Baruzi's famous talk on the completion of his major study of Saint John of the Cross. Another friend of the house was Père Gillet, soon to become General of the Dominicans. Sometimes there were visitors from abroad, such as Miss Brunk, Emeritus Professor of Romance Languages at Swarthmore College, on whom Mademoiselle Zanta's ideas must have made a deep impression.

In 1928 Bergson was awarded the Nobel Prize, and Mademoiselle Zanta wrote an article of congratulation in the *Nouvelles Littéraires*. In thanking her Bergson said that her article explained 'if not what he had done, at least what he would have liked to do.'

Like her other friends, Père Teilhard was aware of the demands her immensely productive, busy life made on her, and the efforts she had to make to remain at other people's service. She made it a point of duty to answer all letters and advise all those who came to her with their problems; indeed she tried to impart an energy at times lacking in herself. Her writing, and her practice of keeping her notebooks up to date, extended far into the nights. The time came when she began to feel an insidious fatigue gaining on her; something in the springs of her being was slackening.

'I'm under pressure,' she wrote to a friend. 'I'm working like a Trojan. I take delight in these high ideas, but I'm worried at not having enough time. May God grant me the generous gift of time, was Saint Augustine's prayer. It's mine too.'

And as she observed that her strength was diminishing, she murmured as if in a low voice, 'God has given us our life of work, a heavy yet sweet burden; I say heavy because my strength is failing, but I add sweet because of the matchless joys it has given me.'

She had in mind, particularly, her major study of

Vittoria Colonna, which she started in 1925, worked at for seventeen years, but was never able to finish. It was a magnificent project. Time and again Père Teilhard encouraged her to set boldly out on the high seas of this work without getting too much bogged down over the documentation. But she only intensified her research: she visited libraries in Rome; in 1928 she went to Florence and Naples, while her exploration of the Vatican coincided with Pius XI's Jubilee Year. She was enraptured by Rome and soon became familiar with the city, the streets, the people. She would have liked to stay there.

And she knew how to convey its unique atmosphere: 'The old stones of the Claudian aqueduct are lit up with purple glimmers under a stormy sky. And if at that moment a flock of sheep led by a single shepherd passes by, then the symbolism becomes marvellously clear. The past leads, by a long line of great men, martyrs and saints, to the indestructible and universal sheepfold on the Vatican: the ascent through the centuries towards Peter's hill whose shepherd to-day bears the bishop's crook and mitre instead of the staff.'

Mademoiselle Zanta loved travelling, getting to know new places and renewing old impressions. She delighted in nature, country life and work in the fields. She had her favourite ports of call. At the beginning of the holidays she would stay at the lovely manor of la Voulte above the Loire, with her friend Madame de Polignac. At la Voulte there was a well-stocked library and, as she was generally respected and appreciated, working conditions were excellent. Another of her favourite places was Le Chambon, the estate of Marguerite Teillard. The house nestled in the green hilly country of the Cantal, near the Lioran. She loved its tough race of peasants, whose sheer hard work she described in an article 'A travers la mon-

tagne.' I recall spending a summer there with her and
how naturally she fitted into the landscape and way
of life. Then, before autumn settled in, she would
go to friends in the Gironde, or to her family home in
Chantilly.

But she also loved foreign travel. Sometimes she joined
Madame Le Masson in Switzerland and called on Bergson
at Vevey; sometimes she set out for Spain with Madame
Darcanne. In 1930 she crossed that peninsula from north
to south. Her stay at Montserrat filled her with delight.
But she herself never referred to an occasion which her
travelling companion was unable to forget. One evening
at Granada, as she was crossing the hotel lounge for sup-
per, everyone rose in silent homage to her great charm
and striking beauty.

On the threshold of sixty Mademoiselle Zanta still
retained a fine poise which was deeply admired by everyone who knew the price she paid to achieve it. She
seemed to have attained the idea she expressed in her
Psychologie du Féminisme: 'A woman's life is a work of
art, a work that calls at every moment for inspiration
and discipline.'

Meanwhile Père Teilhard was continuing with his discovery of the world, and first and foremost of China.
He had spent much time meditating, reflecting, writing;
he had already written the first draft of *Le Milieu Divin*.
His method of thought and the main lines of his vision
were now very clear. And though one was accustomed
to vast speculations in Mademoiselle Zanta's little salon,
never before had such cosmic views been heard
there.

He was now a man both simplified and magnified,
who could ask himself questions about things usually considered banal and commonplace. Problem and mystery

were born of daily events and ordinary encounters. '[. . .] Air and sea,' he wrote, 'a thick, living envelope, in which life swarms and hovers, as fluid and dense as the medium that holds it. Astonishment before the shape and the wonderful flight of the gull: how was that craft built? The worst failing of our minds is that we fail to see the really big problems simply because the forms in which they arise are right under our eyes. How many gulls have I seen, how many other people have seen them, without giving a thought to the mystery that accompanies their flight?'[1]

He perceived the extent to which 'his inner life was dominated by the twin peaks of boundless faith in Our Lord as animator of the world, and a pure faith in the world (especially the human world) as animated by God.'

He believed emphatically in the future of the world, in that slow progress by which mankind is making its way towards unity, a sense of fraternity, and love. The world, being a thought of God, cannot end up in failure, cannot misfire. Everything is fulfilled in Christ. The importance of the person is essential; each person should work according to the deepest current in his being, in his soul, and should thus unite himself with God's creative act and be possessed by the immense joy of creation.

Mademoiselle Zanta enthusiastically embraced Teilhard's thought which was at once fearless, lofty and charitable, calling us always to a great hope and a fuller love. She commented, questioned, clarified—in fact played her part in the building of the magnificent edifice.

I myself grew more and more interested in the development of his thought, in the orientation of his mind, in

[1] *Letters from a Traveller*, London, Collins, and New York, Harper and Row, 1962, p. 123.

his words charged with such strange power, in the whole
intellectual and spiritual ascent of the scientist, priest and
poet.

It was a wonderful experience to see him in discussion,
to note both the tone and the direction of his thought.
He was so deeply aware of the infinite diversity of souls,
and he knew so well that each person has his own individual way of approaching reality and seeking truth,
that it was very important to him not to misrepresent
anything nor offend anyone. For him discussion was
never a dialectical game aimed at refuting an opponent,
much less catching him out in his own arguments. What
mattered was to convince, lay hold of the core of truth
in all thought, and freely expound his own inner conviction. He wanted his interlocutor, too, to reveal
himself as frankly as possible. He listened, had the knack
of grasping the other's line of thought, followed its
development step by step; and when he pressed him to
go further, he pushed him in the direction of his (his
interlocutor's) own thought, inviting him to remain true
to himself as he advanced, certain that there would be
convergence at a given moment. He was warm, encouraging, affirmative, appreciative, and if he gained
mastery in the end it was as though unwillingly.

And when on other occasions Père Teilhard expounded
his thought to student audiences, he liked to put before
them a vast synthesis in which his enthusiasm could find
full vent: the universe confronts us like some wonderful
prey for the blessed flight of the soul, the whole universe
to be loved, to be baptised. For surely we are surrounded
by resplendent evidence of human energy and human
love. 'There exists, outside the Church, an immense
quantity of goodness and beauty which will certainly
only be fulfilled in Christ; but, meanwhile, it exists,
and we must feel a fellowship with it if we want to

be fully Christian and if we want to assimilate it to
God.'

Yes, he said, there is certainly progress, but we mustn't
think of it in an over-simplified way; a virtuous and
noble pagan considered it in no way extraordinary to
keep slaves; whereas to-day, whatever the reality of our
feelings and the state of our hearts, no one would dare
to mention slavery. . . . There we have an example of
progress on the unending road of man's endeavour.

Once again came departure, great distances, solitude—
followed, again, by returns. At their meetings Mademoiselle Zanta and Père Teilhard had just time to tell
one another of new orientations in their thought. It was
especially at the approach of evening that a great sense
of spiritual nakedness fell on them both. Both recognised
this at their meeting in 1938—their last—as Père Teilhard
was detained in China during the whole of the second
world war.

For all the weariness that overwhelmed her, Mademoiselle Zanta carried on with her arduous work as usual,
and in 1934 and 1935 we still find her giving lectures in
philosophy; first on Bergson's *Two Sources of Morality
and Religion*, and the following year on the problem of
God in Bergson and Blondel. Bergson was delighted
when he knew how wholeheartedly she tried to interpret
his final work. 'I know,' he wrote to her, 'that the subject
it deals with has always been in the forefront of your
preoccupations.'

She was hard put to it towards the end to fulfil all her
obligations: her teaching, her article-writing, her student
receptions never gave her a moment's respite. She lamen-
ted that she could not find the time needed for 'Vittoria
Colonna,' but struggled on. She had not chosen her task;
she must bear the burden to the end. Yet little by little
she was forced to give up nearly everything that made

up her life's work: her lectures and her lessons (she had again taken up regular teaching). Her strength gave out, and for five years she had no respite from pain. Along this upward path of suffering she made new friends.

In her *Psychologie du Féminisme* she had written that the greatest geniuses among women were saints such as Joan of Arc and Catherine of Siena. And it was with two saints that she passed these final years: Saint Odile and Saint Monica. To them she devoted her two last books.

With Saint Odile she was able to rediscover the Alsace of her family and youth. She was happy to get back to Strasburg, Obernai and the Holy Mountain, and it was up there that she discovered the great Abbess Odile, 'God's sun.' She invoked her as a peace-maker at the frontier of two countries, two peoples.

Two of the last years of her suffering she devoted to Saint Monica, and when the book appeared in 1941 it was generally felt that in attempting to plumb the meditation of the mother, and the soul and struggle of Saint Augustine, she had raised herself up and fulfilled herself at last.

Her nature now seemed sublimated by a mysterious transformation. To outward appearances she seemed as alert and lively as ever, she overflowed with advice and kindness to others, she had the same vital spark; but she was now possessed by a new kind of solitude. She had once said: 'Our face fades, our physical strength fails, and the personality affirms itself. It creates solitude, and what grandeur there is in this solitude!'

Her family and friends were around her, lavishing their devotion on her, and she herself paid tribute to this virtue of friendship: 'God, who knows his ever-anxious creature, ever-distrustful of herself and with insufficient faith and resignation to abandon herself wholly to him, has happily given her incomparable friends to sustain her in her life.' They were all there: her nephew and niece, Marguerite Teillard, Madame Darcanne, Maurice Donnay, dear old Abbé Mugnier. Bergson, now paralysed, was no longer able to visit the Avenue de Madrid. She went to see him for the last time on April 24, 1938: they had a long talk about which, however, she never spoke. In the concluding days of her life Père Sertillanges was also in attendance to give her support.

She was still the worker of good-will who never withheld her contribution to the common effort. 'There is so much to be done, the world is so corrupt, that a tiny labourer such as myself should never lose a moment in trying to pour into it a little good—so little! But the intention is there, and God can turn it into a great good.'

And she wrote to a friend: 'I am far too taken up with my own petty affairs and not enough with the big affair. I thought it over at Mass this morning and reproached myself heartily. It is absolutely vital that I turn over a new leaf and make some slight moral progress. We are going further and further along the road that leads to God, and yet I'm not jettisoning the baggage that obscures my sight of him. I want to work to unburden myself of this cumbersome self that I sense wherever I turn. . . . We must not erect a screen between our personality and the divine impulse.'

In 1941 she wrote to a woman friend who was ill as she was: 'I pray with you, and I hear the same cry everywhere repeated as it rises, from the Cross of Jesus and from the crosses we ourselves have to bear, upwards to Our Father's heart. Hope is born in me anew, I live in his arms, I rest my head on his adorable heart and I await the resurrection. It will come; let us keep faith and hope ever-present in our hearts, and let us always love more and better. What will suffering matter when we see him

whom we love, when we contemplate him face to face,
when we are altogether his? . . . Live a little in heaven
while you do your purgatory on earth.'

To another friend she said, 'Thank God with me. At
the moment I am inundated by his grace. I still have the
better part.'

Pentecost was her 'season of light.' Every time this
feast came round she exclaimed, 'I will pray to the Spirit
to inspire me, the Spirit of light, the Spirit of peace, the
Spirit of strength; I love this feast so much.'

It was in this spirit, and having followed her lifelong
vocation to the end, that she left her family and friends.

For the drawing up of these few facts concerning
Mademoiselle Zanta, I am much indebted to the un-
published biography written by her best friend, Madame
Darcanne. While re-reading her book, which its author
showed me while she was engaged on it, I can only hope
that the manuscript will one day be published, as it is so
important for the light it throws on the French feminist
movement between the years 1900 and 1940. A whole
epoch is brought to life.

Mademoiselle Léontine Zanta published the following
works:

La renaissance du stoïcisme au XVIe siècle, thesis for her
doctorat ès lettres, Champion, 1914.

La traduction française du Manuel d'Epictète d'André de
Rivaudeau au XVIe siècle, published with an Introduction
by Léontine Zanta, Paris, Champion, 1914.

L'activité féminine de demain, Paris, Revue des Jeunes, 1919.

Psychologie du Féminisme, preface by Paul Bourget, Paris,
4th ed., Plon, 1922.

La science et l'amour, novel, Paris, Plon, 1921.

La part du feu, novel, Paris, Plon, 1927.

Sainte-Odile, Paris, Flammarion, 'Les pèlerinages' series, 1931.

Sainte Monique et son fils. La mère chrétienne, preface by A.-D. Sertillanges, Paris, Plon, 1941.

The Trial of Faith

HENRI DE LUBAC, S.J.

Thirteen years have elapsed since the death of Père Teilhard de Chardin; more than twenty-six since that of Léontine Zanta. Since the time when they corresponded, a whole world has been swallowed up. So we may be allowed to suppose that there is no risk of indiscretion in publishing these letters. Indeed, from several points of view, publication may well seem opportune. Numbers of books and essays have drawn attention not only to Père Teilhard's thought, but also to his private life and feelings; some of which have at times failed to respect the reality of the facts or provide a sufficiently informed interpretation of them. A document such as the following, the importance of which is manifest, will enable the reader to form a more exact picture on a number of crucial points.

M. Robert Garric has already said all that is essential about Léontine Zanta and her relations with Père Teilhard. Nevertheless, as these letters contain numerous allusions to Père Teilhard's personal position both as regards his Order or, more generally, as regards the Church, the editor thought it might be advisable to add some clarifications about decisive incidents between the years 1924 and 1938.[1]

---

[1] Besides the letters here published, we have made use of letters addressed to Père Auguste Valensin and to ourself; as well as of Claude Cuénot: *Pierre Teilhard de Chardin* (Burns Oates, 1965) (Eng. ed.), and René d'Ouince, s.j.: *L'épreuve de l'obéissance dans la vie du Père Teilhard de Chardin* in *L'homme devant Dieu*, vol. III, pp. 331-446 (in the *Théologie* series, Aubier, 1964).

Until November, 1924, there was no serious crisis directly involving Père Teilhard. He had long known that his 'evolutionism', far from being accepted by all, earned him a certain amount of distrust. He was not unaware that the spiritual experience described in his *Écrits du temps de la guerre* (*Writings in Time of War*)[1] was uncommon in the Church and that there was a certain uneasiness here and there among his intimates. Equally he was painfully conscious of the 'cumbersome, narrow and outmoded' elements in the Catholic society of his time, so much so that they caused him deep inner distress and he sometimes cried out '*Cupio dissolvi.*' During the summer of 1920 he had suffered on behalf of his friends, Pierre Charles, Auguste Valensin and Joseph Huby, when, on the injunction of Cardinal Merry del Val, then Secretary of the Holy Office, their Superior General had proscribed in the severest terms the doctrine of Père Rousselot, known as that of 'the eyes of faith.' For Teilhard it was an alarming symptom. Some presentiment of what lay ahead occurs in a letter he wrote to Père Auguste Valensin round about this time: 'The worst thing that could happen to *me* would be to be sent off to some distant land where in fact it would suit me very well to go and research and work.' But as the tone of this remark shows, though he found the atmosphere menacing, it was not yet tragic.

Then, suddenly, it became so. In 1920 Père Teilhard had been appointed lecturer in geology at the Institut Catholique in Paris. In 1922 he was awarded his Doctorate of Science after a brilliant oral examination. In 1923-24 he obtained leave of absence so as to accompany his colleague, Père Licent, on a scientific expedition into Northern China and Mongolia; it was then that he wrote his *Mass on the World*, whose rather solemn enthusiasm re-

[1] Collins' London, and Harper & Row, New York, 1968.

veals the ardent but serene mysticism typical of that period of his life. He was back in Paris in October, 1924. On November 13 he received an urgent letter from his Provincial, Père Costa de Beauregard, summoning him to Lyons. The first crisis had begun.

Two years previously, at the request of a colleague who was professor of Dogmatics (all his life Teilhard was besieged by requests of this kind, to which he responded reluctantly, as he thought that 'papers along the lines of "The Phenomenon of Man" would be much more useful than discussions about Adam and Eve'), he had drawn up a note, inspired partly by his discussions with Père Charles, in which he indicated three possible directions 'for research into a representation of original sin.' They were, he pointed out, no more than 'very approximative orientations, and certainly not viable as they are.' Now in some mysterious way this text ended up in Rome. The censors who examined it proved severe, and the authorities no less so. 'They want me to promise in writing that I will never *say* or write anything against the traditional position of the Church on original sin.' Hence, anguish of conscience:

It's both too vague and too absolute. I feel I should, in conscience, reserve for myself (1) the right to carry on research with professional men (*ex jure naturali*); (2) the right to bring help to the disturbed and troubled (*ex jure sacerdotali*). I am hoping to be able to get the formula they are asking me to sign altered into something of this kind: 'I bind myself not to spread (not to carry on proselytism for) the particular explanations contained in my note.'

This affair cast its shadow over the whole of 1925. New censors were appointed. Despite the efforts of Mgr Baudrillart, his rector at the Institut Catholique, and those of his immediate superiors, Roman rigour showed no relaxation. Finally he had to subscribe to six propositions of which only one, in last analysis, caused him real difficulty, though he resigned himself to signing it on the advice of his counsellors. After that he had to leave once more for China, this time as an exile. He never reappeared in Paris as a teacher. He took the blow badly. He wrote to Père Valensin on May 16, 1925:

Dear friend, please help me. I've put a good face on it outwardly, but within it is something that resembles an agony or a storm. I think I see that, if I separated myself off, or kicked over the traces in any way whatsoever (humanly speaking, it would be so simple and so 'easy'), I would be disloyal to my faith in Our Lord's animation of everything that happens, and in His own value, superior to that of all the elements of this world. Moreover I would be compromising . . . the religious value of my ideas. People would see it as turning my back on the Church, as pride, who knows what? It is essential that I should show, by my example, that if my ideas seem innovations, they nevertheless make me as faithful as anyone to the old attitude. That's what I think I see. But even here, there are shadows . . .

Henceforward his life was dogged by external difficulties and disappointments which formed an almost endless web around him. There were plans for returning to Europe that turned out abortive. There was the threat of being buried in Beirut where he would have 'nothing to teach or find.' And, after a series of vain hopes, there was the impossibility of publishing Le Milieu Divin, which was stopped by Rome in extremis. There were censorship troubles that even blocked a study on Transformism. On December 30, 1929, he wrote:

Not another word from Louvain about Le Milieu Divin, which should have gone to press in July (I was expecting some 'hitch' at the last moment in that quarter). As for my article on Transformism (which was approved and requested by Dopp and Maréchal) it was stopped irreversibly by the diocesan censorship of Malines. Some suspicious canon riddled it with question- and exclamation-marks. Dopp wrote me a broken-hearted letter. I took the whole thing philosophically. But all the same this tenacious and persistent obstructionism is infinitely wearing. . . .

Soon afterwards he ran into similar obstacles over a new study on the Phenomenon of Man. Then came the troubles of his friend Édouard Le Roy; he was deeply distressed when four of Le Roy's books were put on the Index and the author was forced to make a 'recantation.' On such occasions, he confided to Auguste Valensin, 'we feel the loss of Léonce [i.e. Père de Grandmaison who had died in 1927] all the more deeply.' Then he himself was yet again delated to Rome. He was forbidden to allow his name to go forward for the Collège de France. He felt the weight of suspicion unceasingly upon him, and for a time he had grounds for fearing that he would be requested to formulate new 'propositions.' And over and above what happened to him personally, he suffered when he saw an 'integrist' mentality spreading, which before had been merely the prerogative of an aggressive party; 'integrism' tended, as he put it, 'to identify Christian orthodoxy with respect for the tiniest wheels of a little microcosm constructed centuries ago,' while his own ideal, 'the true Christian ideal,' was 'integralism, namely the extension of the Christian directives to all the resources contained in the world.' Without really realising how bold some of his own ideas could seem, he suffered equally from the narrow vision within which his superiors seemed confined—whose frequent ignorance of the real problems, coupled with a desire to play safe, risked throwing them into the arms of their most backward advisers. Thus more than once he was told, with a view to checking his impetus, that he belonged to an Order of 'conservatives,' not 'pioneers.' He even received a letter laying down what should be his line of conduct: 'The Catholic scientist has an infallible rule which spares him many wasted labours: he must dismiss *a priori* all that contradicts Catholic dogma.' Though he recognised the kind intentions of this letter, it seemed to him to bear witness to a 'profound lack of understanding'; it confused the planes of science and faith as though divine revelation had 'ever legitimately dispensed man from the effort of research'; 'as if,' as he was to put it later, 'in the field of experiment we could make use (from the same point of view and for the same facts) of two different sources of light: that of the Found and that of the Taught.' Much more than that, and, as must be admitted, not unreasonably, he saw in the rule propounded to him an ill-omened interdict laid, in the name of dogma, on any idea of evolution.

These facts have been summarised so that the reader may understand some of the judgments expressed by Père Teilhard in his letters, and the quality of the emotions they disclose; better still, so that he may be able to appreciate more fully Père Teilhard's fidelity to his priestly vocation within both the Church and the Society of Jesus.

As he himself puts it, he had to give the Fire its share.[1] What does this mean? His thought which, professionally, bore on the vastest aggregates, led him to recognise the enormous share of contingency implicit in the concrete existence, *hic et nunc* and in all their particularities, both of a religious Order and of the Church herself. Experience showed him not so much their all-too-human but

[1] The allusion is to Mlle Zanta's novel, *La part du feu*, Paris, Plon, 1927.

'transitory' pettinesses, which he did not want to see, but their purely human 'littleness.' On all this aspect of things, to which he perhaps at times paid too much attention, he judged freely. He accepted like a man the tensions resulting therefrom when there seemed evidence of a providential inevitability about them. But he would never agree to stand aside. And if, as regards his Order and the Church, he no longer felt 'that sort of naïve and filial attachment which is doubtless the treasure of many,' he remained just as strongly attached to them, but for 'new and higher reasons.' With a more aware sort of realism he appreciated their 'wonderful treasure of religious experience' and their 'unique power of divinisation'; and the new kind of bond that was the outcome, if less instinctive, was no less deep nor, in last analysis, less 'cordial.'

His loyalty to the Society of Jesus was complete. 'The faintest idea of a move to leave the Order has never crossed my mind,' he wrote in 1929. And he retained the same basic attitude in the years that followed. He insisted on staying in constant and trusting contact with all his superiors. He made no plan of any importance without consulting them, and made no decision without their full approval. He never remotely concealed his bold flights of thought from them—he sought out every opportunity for discussing his ideas with them and expounding the great design of his apostolate. As we shall see, he never abandoned the effort and the hope—sometimes rather naïve—of convincing them.

Fidelity to his Order was only one of the forms of his fidelity to the Church. The problem confronting him first and foremost was a problem of sincerity. We can hear an echo of this in his recommendation to Léontine Zanta, in 1927, never to 'let go of these two threads: loyalty towards ourselves, and attachment to the Church.'

And he added: 'Pray that I may never break either of them.' And, two years later, he wrote to Père Valensin: 'I am more and more determined henceforward to be *true*, without any compromise or diplomacy. If Our Lord is as great as we believe him to be, he will be able to guide my effort in such a way that there is no breaking-point.' And so in fact things turned out. Sometimes the threads were stretched to the utmost; but nothing ever broke. If to-day we can quote his harshest views without causing scandal, it is because he never gave way to the easy (and always superficial) game of agitation and pamphleteering, nor to bitter recriminations. He said without mincing his words what he thought he saw, but he said it privately, to his soul's confidants or to his superiors in a genuine examination of conscience. If excess is sometimes to be found here, this is because his suffering at times became almost intolerable, and because of the perhaps rather uni-lateral way in which he saw things owing to his very desire for universality (a fault which the conditions of his life could only reinforce). But, at the basis of every-thing, we always find the purest and most disinterested concern of the apostle. Thus, in the analysis he made in 1926, 'We are no longer "Catholic," in fact; but we are defending a system, a sect.' Or yet again, in 1929, in what may well be the harshest judgment he ever made:

> . . . the only thing that I can be: a voice that repeats, *opportune et importune*, that the Church will waste away so long as she does not escape from the factitious world of verbal theology, of quantitative sacramentalism, and over-refined devotions in which she is enveloped, so as to reincarnate herself in the real aspirations of mankind. . . . Of course I can see well enough what is paradoxical in this attitude: if I need Christ and the Church I should accept Christ as he is presented by the

Church, with its burden of rites, administration and
theology. That's what you'll tell me, and I've often
said it to myself. But now I can't get away from the
evidence that the moment has come when the Christian
impulse should 'save Christ' from the hands of the
clerics so that the world may be saved.

The clerics he is speaking of, we need hardly say, are
those whose narrowness and blindness he had experienced
at close quarters. He got the impression that there were
certain 'occupants of the pulpit of Moses' whose entire
intellectual activity 'goes backwards and forwards in a
field of thought that most modern people have abandoned,' and who insist that others remain in the same
closed circle. He was thinking of the speakers and writers
whose 'dead prose' is never brought to life by any 'religious sap,' and in whom only 'truths already digested a
hundred times and with no living essence' are to be
found. These formed a block with the many who
nourished 'the secret hope that the nineteenth century
will be wiped out and we shall soon find ourselves back
in the good old pre-scientific and pre-revolutionary
days.' Many of them might well be 'firm believers';
but in some more or less confused way they 'are waiting
for a *retreat into the past*' whereas, whether we like it or
not, 'we are moving towards an ever newer world of
man.' So he came to see them all as a menace. 'Should
this spirit prevail, it would be the final disaster and the
consummation of the schism with mankind. 'It is impossible,' he concluded, 'that this should happen. But
happen it will if we do not fight.'

Here, obviously, we are dealing with language that
will never obtain everyone's approval, for there are
others in the Church who see everything from a different
point of view. Even inasmuch as we may agree with it,
the wording no longer corresponds with our present

situation. But however that may be, these are not the
words of a man whose faith is wavering, a man of little
belief or little love. 'I dream,' he said, 'of seeing the
Church really beautiful and beyond attack.' Even this
sounds too negative. He expressed his ideal vision of
Christianity better in a text dated June, 1926—we can
leave to others the task of assessing to what extent this
vision is chimerical. We ourselves find its inspiration lofty
and generous and also, in general terms, in conformity
with both historical reality and the thought of some of
the greatest men in the Catholic tradition:

> Christianity now appears to me much less a closed
> and established whole than an axis of progression and
> assimilation. Apart from this axis, I cannot see any
> guarantee or any way out for the world. But around
> this axis, I can glimpse an immense quantity of truths
> and attitudes for which orthodoxy has not yet made
> room. If I dared use a word which could be given in-
> acceptable meanings, I feel myself irreducibly 'hyper-
> Catholic.'

During the somewhat strained, but on the whole more
peaceful years that he had spent in Paris between his
return from the war and the crisis that broke out in 1924,
he had already had keen experience of the paradox that
he was later to feel all the time: 'I feel bound, by my very
substance, to an organism whose unwarranted narrowness and irrelevance I am perpetually aware of.' But he
had also defined in serene terms what was to be his consistent attitude to the Church:

> I feel two things simultaneously, that Our Lord is
> truly and uniquely in his Church, and that he is at
> the same time something very different (*idem, sed ultra*)
> from what we are told. It is impossible to reach him
> other than by going forward through the mists, that
> is to say by becoming more and more one body with

the Church. But it is also impossible not to want to see his face revealed more fully.

'The trouble with letters is that they often convey the impressions of one moment only—and of only one part of the soul at that moment.' This remark of Père Teilhard's could be addressed to the contemporary reader as he is brought by this book into the intimacy of an extremely free correspondence—whose secrets the author could never have imagined would be available to everyone half a century later. The wording is not always strictly weighed, and naturally more space is given to the expression of the most acute difficulties than to the realities of everyday life. We have taken the remark quoted above to heart so as to avoid as far as possible the danger he hints at. This is why, from among the confidences he lavished on several of his correspondents, we have tried in the main to retain those that express the real constants of his soul. And we find the affirmation of these constants, in the period covered by the letters to Léontine Zanta, through the oscillations between anxiety and serenity through which he passed.

When, on November 13, 1924, he first heard of the blow that was to fall on him, his first reaction was one of total faith; so much so that that very night he was able to write: 'At heart I am at perfect peace. Even this is a manifestation of Our Lord and one of his operations. So why worry?' But he soon became the victim of endless disquieting thoughts. He asked for help, and brotherly help came, and the inner struggle ended—as Claude Cuénot puts it—in a 'spiritual victory.' It was now August, 1925, and he said: 'I see now more clearly and concretely that nothing spiritual, nothing divine, can reach a Christian—or a religious—save through the intermediary of the Church—or of his Order. And my deeper "realisation" of this fundamental truth has certainly made me feel better.' And: 'Now more explicitly and more concretely than before the "crisis" . . . I believe in, and love, the Church, as "mediatrix" between God and the world. And this, I feel, is giving me a good deal of peace.' Yet the victory was not conclusive. In the last months before his exile, while in the midst of his preparations, 'flashes of rebellion' sometimes took hold of him. But after his arrival in Tientsin, in June 1926, he again felt at peace: 'all anger and bitterness are falling away.' When such feelings arose he turned them, 'as best he could,' into 'total sacrifice to Our Lord.' It was then, between November 1926 and March 1927, that he wrote *Le Milieu Divin*. Despite a certain 'state of intellectual and moral dissatisfaction,' which did not affect him deep down, he was able to write, 'I feel at ease in the hands of Our Lord.'

The recurrence of such painful incidents made his position more and more uncomfortable, and he underwent further onslaughts of temptation—though, yet again, the inner depths of his soul were not touched. The year 1928, and the early months of 1929, seem to have been at moments exceptionally hard. Père Teilhard admitted before long that he had experienced bouts of 'anti-ecclesiasticism' and almost 'anti-Christianity' that he found hard to control. Sometimes, he said, 'I no longer knew what firm and shaken [=unshaken?] elements there remained in the depths of my being.' An essay on *Le Sens humain* which he wrote on the boat on his way back to China after a few months' stay in France (it is dated Ceylon, February 12, 1929) alarmed Père Valensin, and Teilhard himself declared soon afterwards that he would like 'to erase that hint of bitterness deriving from transitory attitudes now left behind.' And so once again 'the dust settled,' peace was restored, everything melted into 'a wider and more serene awareness.' He attributed this to

God's goodness and the prayers of his friends. It was following this pattern that he emerged from each of his crises: with the conviction that thanks to the crisis he had managed to Christianise some new province of his inner being, and, 'with God's help' he always returned to 'the deep Christian axis.' Each time he was able to end up with: 'I am at peace, and truly, with the Church as with God.'

On April 2, 1929, he wrote to Père Valensin: 'My only strength and my "vocation" lie in *synthesising* (more or less satisfactorily!) love of the world and love of the Church'; and already on December 31, 1926, and even more clearly, he had written: 'Instinctively, and especially in the last ten years, I have always offered myself to Our Lord as a sort of testing-ground, where, on a small scale, He might bring about the fusion between the two great loves, of God and the world—for without that fusion I am convinced that no Kingdom of God is possible.' Such was the essence of his programme to the end. He conceived it and maintained it in terms of a prayer of offering. It encouraged him, gave him patience, and reassured him, even in days of storm and stress. As he knew full well, a testing ground does not always yield entirely successful results. And even successes cannot always be translated immediately into perfect formulas. He himself was always appealing for advice, controls, correctives, without always being able to accept them as right. He modestly asked to be 'made use of and canalised.' So, on deeper reflection, he can hardly have been all that surprised at the cautious behaviour of his superiors. 'It is possible that my destiny lies in living, right to the end, on the fringe of official ideas and attitudes.' Yet under the impulse of his Catholic feelings, and following his doctrine that the beneficial part played by the 'passivities' must be acknowledged only when every possible effort has been made, he went on: 'But I wouldn't like to leave anything undone, on my side, that could put an end to this situation.' It was for this reason that he wanted so much to see *Le Milieu Divin* approved by higher authority: ' . . . so that I may feel with greater certainty that the spirit of the Church is with me.' And he needed so little to have his confidence restored! In the final months of 1926 he learnt through the newspapers of several declarations made by the government of Pius XI:

> One of the things that has given me comfort recently has been noticing the wider and more universalising tendencies in Rome. So far it's only been a matter of policies and material evangelisation. But the impetus may already have been given. And then I tell myself that I may be less on the fringe of the *'sentire cum Ecclesia'* than I had feared, or than I had been led to think.

'It seems to me,' he said in 1929, 'that they could do anything they like with me *through trust*.' Such obviously sincere reflections as these must surely be encouraging to those who have any part in authority. Or again in 1933: 'It's tiresome, as I wrote to Père de Bonneville, that they make no attempt in Rome to see what is constructive and conservative in my effort.' Then, referring to a new denunciation against him: 'Whatever my accusers may think, people outside are not deceived about it; and though I may give the impression of being somewhat unclerical, I don't think anyone has thought me "of little faith".' Hence the idea which he formulated as early as December 31, 1926, and which was to crop up periodically—but was only fulfilled at last, and unsuccessfully, in the autumn of 1948—of a 'visit *ad limina*.'[1]

> Do you consider it impossible that some day I should go to Rome (without a rope round my neck) to try to

[1] i.e. to Rome (Tr..)

make them understand in the right quarter the sort of evangelisation I feel called to, and by what methods I'm trying to speak and understand (too well, perhaps . . .) the language of people as remote from us as the Chinese, and more interesting even? I want to be left free to talk to them. But in this business there is a question of rites, that is of words, raised by people who know nothing about the real meaning of the debate. But still, I'd very much like to try to do something in Rome—to make them see what I see. . . .

What he sees . . .: he describes it and makes no bones about it, and here too lies a 'danger' in his letters—for we come across formulations that did not shock his correspondents who knew him well, because they knew exactly what he was getting at; but if they were to be taken out of context and artificially strung together, they could establish a 'Teilhardism'—or a 'pseudo-Teilhardism'—that might well be condemned.

To be sure, anyone who interpreted the words he wrote to Léontine Zanta—that he saw the future 'all ablaze with God springing up everywhere'—as some sort of 'evolutionist pantheism' would have to be totally ignorant of his thought, and blind to the perfectly orthodox explanations that he repeatedly gave to such formulations. No such misapprehension could possibly have occurred to his correspondent. Or again, when he says that he prefers the word 'Diaphany' to the word 'Epiphany,' it is enough to remember that he is speaking for us, to-day, who are no longer expecting a new and special manifestation of God on earth; and he had just been writing in *Le Milieu Divin* that the Diaphany in question could only be properly understood through the one and unique Epiphany on which it depends. 'The immense enchantment of the divine milieu owes all its concrete value in the long run to the human-divine contact which was revealed in the Epiphany of Jesus.' He repeated that again and again. When he speaks, in his own kind of shorthand, of loving 'nothing but the earth' (or, in the same way, 'nothing but man'), only a fool would read Nietzschean echoes into it! In this formula the earth is not being contrasted with heaven, but with a too-small Europe, indeed with petty nationalism—the nationalism, as he himself put it, of the *Écho de Paris*.[1]

More serious uneasiness might be aroused by an assertion such as this: 'If I was less deeply inserted within the Church, I would be less equipped for the work of setting her free.' Yet only an inattentive reader, or a malicious one, could denounce this as an admission of a secret tactic, similar to the one for which (rightly or wrongly) certain Modernists were reproached. His insertion within the Church meant for Teilhard his very fidelity, and he knew what this demanded. He had not only to obey in an external way, but to pray, renounce himself and sanctify himself, so as to merit however small a hearing; and as for the freedom he dreamt of, it was the very opposite of taking a step outside the faith! Much later, replying to a priest who had left the Church, he said that it was better 'to work for reform from within,' and he never abandoned his task of reform or liberation as undertaken in close union with the responsible heads of the Church. His attitude was the very opposite of the one adopted by some of the Modernists at one time—just as his realism about the Incarnation was the very opposite of their doctrine. He had always and unequivocally thought of the advances that he wanted as having to be achieved 'on the Roman stem, taken in its integrality.' It was only on this condition that he agreed to speak of a 'neo-Christian-

[1] The influential French daily in the twenties and thirties. It took a nationalist line but was totally unconnected with the *Action Française*, which took an extreme nationalist and eventually pro-Nazi line (Tr.).

ity': an expression we may well be permitted to view as unfortunate but which meant, for him, nothing other than the full Christianisation of 'neo-humanism' whose dawn he glimpsed before most of his contemporaries. The crisis of man in our century offers 'really extraordinary features': the world is renewing itself under our very eyes, whatever those 'who forbid it to move' may think or do; Christ should not be linked with 'disappearing forms' . . . And if we have to take more care than in the past not to represent the divinity in the guise of 'a great "neolithic" landowner,' this in no way means suppressing or toning down God's personal characteristics—the very opposite. Nothing was nearer to his heart than establishing and promoting faith in a personal God.

However, the letters to Léontine Zanta do not only deal with crises and rash projects! Apart from information of every kind that they provide about Père Teilhard and his milieu, they also constitute—like the letters to Marguerite Teillard during the first world war—a true spiritual direction of a conscience. We can see the outline of the 'director's' spirituality through the advice he gives. Its essential principles have been pointed out elsewhere, and they are habitually expressed in such simple and lucid terms that any further commentary would be superfluous. Moreover his expression of them is always discreet. Yet each time it breaks through, it uncovers by its strength the depths of what lies underneath. Thus it could not possibly spring from a mediocre inner life. At the same time as he was leading an extremely active and difficult existence, exploring the planet, scrutinising the past history of earth and man, and their future through their past, involving himself passionately in the battle of ideas, seeking to win over the leaders of his Church to a vision that seemed to him vital, and all the while himself subjected to private struggles and trials whose gravity we have glimpsed at—this man, withdrawn into the core of his soul, was habitually in communion with 'the joy of Being' for which he had been given a 'deep taste'; 'obscurely,' he 'entrenched himself in the feeling that Being is infinitely richer and more renewing than our logic'; he 'renounced' himself in a 'Greater-than-himself.' Having given himself 'into God's hands,' he calmly re-tempered his strength 'in the great and peace-giving intensity of the divine Omnipresence.' He set out again 'on the Ocean of the One Thing Needful.'

The Letters

Editor's Note

This edition of the letters to Mademoiselle Léontine Zanta is reproduced from the originals in Père Teilhard de Chardin's handwriting. It is thanks to the kind permission of the family—who had carefully preserved them—that we are able to publish this important record of the intellectual and spiritual life of the author. Special thanks are due to Madame Roland Guétin, Mademoiselle Zanta's niece.

The text is published in its entirety. The only omissions are six short passages (referred to on each occasion in the footnotes) which deal with a strictly personal matter; to give them publicity would have been both indiscreet and against Père Teilhard's intention—as is plain from the way he writes.

We have reduced the footnotes to an indispensable minimum. For further details readers are referred to *The Making of a Mind* (London, Collins, and New York, Harper & Row, 1965), *Letters from a Traveller* (London, Collins, and New York, Harper & Row, 1962), and above all to Claude Cuénot's book, *Teilhard de Chardin* (London, Burns Oates, and Baltimore, Helicon Press, 1965).

Michel de Certeau

Hautes Études, Race Course Road, Tientsin[1]
Note the address!
May 26, [1923][2]

Dear Mademoiselle,

I was deeply touched to find a letter from you waiting on my table when I arrived here three days ago. To me it was both a sign of welcome and an encouragement to do to the best of my ability the work I have come here to do. For I told you, didn't I, that if I was leaving so many dear friends whom I loved feeling near to me in Paris, it was because I felt I couldn't serve them loyally without following the 'star' that drew me to the Far East. You may be sure that memories of you have followed me here and give me support. You are pre-eminently among those for whose sake I would like to become better—even at the cost of distance.

Your Paris news interested me a lot and will always interest me. I feel a need not to lose contact with that warm spiritual focus in which you occupy so large a place. I have come here to re-immerse myself in those still raw areas of the material and human universe. In this respect I believe that I have, and shall have, all I want, and more. But precisely because I'm now in an incoherent mass of men and things that are very new to me, it is necessary for me to keep in touch with the more luminous and 'spiritualised' areas I have just left—so as not to be swamped, or at least cooled off. Your letters now, like our good talks in the past, will help me and force me not to allow any diminution of my faith in the unity which is God's end for the human effort. One needs

[1] The Jesuit residence in Tientsin.
[2] The year, not included in manuscript, is 1923: Teilhard reached Tientsin on May 23.

to keep a tight hold on this faith, you know, when one
is in the midst of the incredible diversity of man's races
and preoccupations. .... Here in the Far East our Western
philosophy seems as lost as the earth does among the
other stars and planets of the heavens. To tell you the
truth I'd find it very difficult to say what exactly goes
on in the heads of people around the Pacific. One's first
impression is that they're living in a complete state of
prosaic utilitarianism, without any clear ideal or hope. But
this very immersion (*without* subsequent emergence) in
the human '*business*'[1] makes them very remote, very
different, from us, and our inner preoccupations seem
to have made scarcely any impact on them as yet—and
they show no signs of maintaining themselves, of even
developing, in the spirit of those who have come to
evangelise them. Anyway, on one's first arrival here
(though it would be absurd for me to make any final
judgment after three weeks in the Far East) one gets the
impression of going down several degrees in natural
human life. Hence the need which I mentioned just now
to react—so as not to forget and not to have doubts.

During my journey out I often felt a need to remake—
for myself and others—my profession of faith in life as
having a meaning. I discovered the doctor on the *Cor-
dillère*—Dr Béchamp—to be a particularly original and
intelligent man (he's a nephew of Mme Lucie Delarue-
Mardrus; he even helped her to revise that novel about
the Le Havre missionary that you were talking about this
winter. How small the world is!) Dr Béchamp is probably one of the two or three most gifted men I have
met in my life (physicist, linguist, musician, man of
letters—and he carries it all so lightly). The only person
with whom I could compare him is my friend Père

[1] The author's use of an English word is indicated throughout this
edition by italic type in quotation marks (Tr.).

Charles, but a Charles who lacked (or distrusted, so rejected) 'mystical feeling'. We had long conversations nearly every day, and became as close friends as is possible without a common faith. Dr Béchamp believes in the interconnection of things, but doesn't think any certain statement can be made (except by purely subjective choice) regarding their final purpose. By inclination he's a sceptic, and rather disillusioned, and what's more (and in this we were in close sympathy) ferociously impatient about any unjustified yoke over the intelligence. I naturally didn't convert him to my point of view; but I seemed to see clearly that his brilliant and rich nature is unable, at the moment, to provide itself with any rule of behaviour or adequate reason for acting, outside his instinctive taste for intellectual pleasure. Now this instinctive taste, I persist in believing, is not enough to guide and call forth intelligent action. I am more and more persuaded that this dilemma confronts us: either the world is moving towards some universal absolute (in which case it can go on living and progressing), or else such an end doesn't exist (in which case the universe is manifestly *unable to nourish the life it has produced* ever since this life became capable of reflexion and criticism; it is unbreathable and abortive). But I can't agree to admitting that the universe, in its totality, has miscarried, is a '*failure*'. . . . Hence I believe in some Absolute which, *hic et nunc*, is manifested to us only through Christ. As you know, that is my whole system of apologetics. And I can't conceive of any other. I noted that the best unbelievers on our boat—Béchamp or other friends— summed up all ethics in the precept 'don't do to others what you wouldn't want them to do to you.' But, as I see things, this ethical attitude is purely lenitive and static. It lubricates the machinery like oil. This isn't enough. The human machine ought to do more than not

grind. It ought to advance. It requires energy, 'petrol.'
The whole moral problem lies in providing this energy
and 'petrol' (i.e. the obligation to act and the taste for
action). Now I can see no possible source for this apart
from submission to an ideal and universal end (*believed*
and *hoped for*—not tangible—*since it is* universal and yet
to come, whereas we are in the realm of the individual
and the present).

You see that I am again letting myself play the pedant
with you. You know that I do it without 'conceit,' only
so as to talk with you, and tell you what I think, what
I chew over every day. I'd like to know that all is well
with you, physically and morally. Write and think as
much as possible: you need that for your well-being and
so as to do good, and it's the first duty that God has laid
on you, before all the rest. Go on believing absolutely,
without hesitation, that the best sacrifice that you can
offer to Our Lord is the offering of your intelligence and
your activity, so that both may grow as much as possible
—and so that they may find themselves bounded only
where Causes stronger than yourself come in to impose a
divine restriction. I have often told you: the secret of
having peace and never getting stifled (even in the worst
of commonplace circumstances) lies in managing, with
God's help, to perceive the One Element Needful which
circulates in all things, which can give itself to us (with
its joy and freedom) through any object, provided that
object is brought before us by *fidelity* to life, and that
it is transformed by *faith* in the divine presence and
operation.

I expect to be leaving before June 15 for some place or
other in Mongolia. There are brigands pretty well everywhere; but I have an experienced guide.

Goodbye—my thoughts often turn to the little sitting-
room near the balcony from which you can see the sun

setting over the valley of the Seine.[1] There I drew more strength than possibly you know.

Thank you, and faithfully yours *in Christo*,

Teilhard, s.j.

Of course I was delighted by Bremond's success![2]

Beside the Shara-Uso-Gol,
(Eastern Ordos)
August 7, 1923

Dear Mademoiselle,

Thank you for your letter of May 13 which reached me only a week ago. I'm writing to you under canvas (it's raining!) from the most picturesque spot that exists: the bed of a deep ravine close to a Mongol dwelling scooped out in the middle of a table of hardened earth (cut through in the past by the Shara-Uso-Gol). All around are sand-hills and steppes where the horses and sheep pasture beside gazelles, under the distant guard of long-haired, big-booted Mongols. I arrived here, the objective of my journey, by a circuitous route, as we were forced by the drought and the brigands to go round the whole great northern loop of the Hwang-Ho. When I came to China I hardly expected to get much beyond the Great Wall. Yet now I know a large sector of Western Mongolia. I don't regret our six weeks' wandering on mule-back

[1] Number 7, Avenue de Madrid, the flat Mlle Zanta had lived in since 1900. Cf. above p. 14.

[2] The Abbé Henri Bremond had been elected a member of the French Academy on April 19, 1923, taking the place of Mgr Duchesne who had died on April 21, 1922. In answer to the address welcoming him, Bremond devoted a carefully-weighed speech to his predecessor, though one much debated. Cf. *Discours prononcé dans la séance publique tenue par l'Académie française pour la réception de M. l'Abbé Henri Bremond, le jeudi 22 mai 1924.* Institut de France, Paris, *1924,* in 4°, 30 pp.

across mountains and deserts. Not only was there no lack of the picturesque, but as we travelled we came across important—and unexpected—geological and palae-ontological finds, which are probably worth more than all the bones of rhinoceroses, horses and various animals that we are now engaged in extracting from the cliffs of the Shara-Uso-Gol. So we are getting somewhere, and from the scientific point of view I haven't come here in vain. That's the main thing, as regards externals.

But deep down, as you know, the reason why I left Paris for China was to give an example of how I conceive Christian duty—and also to try to become, by means of travel and activity, a better master of my 'faith,' and stronger for putting it forward. On this principal point, I hope I haven't been wasting my time either. Though I have less leisure than during the war, and perhaps less freshness too (the war marked the springtime of my ideas—my intellectual honeymoon), in the last two months I have found myself in similar isolation and confronted with realities equally vast. And both these conditions are eminently favourable for meditating on the great All. Now, in the vast solitudes of Mongolia (which, from the human point of view, are a static and dead region), I see the same thing as I saw long ago at the 'front' (which, from the human point of view, was the most alive region that existed): one single operation is in process of hap-pening in the world, and it alone can justify our action: the emergence of some spiritual Reality, through and across the efforts of life. As I travel on mule-back for whole days on end, I repeat, as in the past—for lack of any other Mass—the 'Mass on the World,' which you already know, and I believe I can say it with still greater clarity and conviction than before. What a beautiful Host this ancient Asia is—a dead Host for the time being (I think)—but bearing, in its dust, the traces of that so long labour from which we are now profiting! As I said to Marguerite,[1] my present impression is not one of being in the bow of a ship (as during the war) but in the stern, leaning over the wake (and seeing the trace of what has passed): and this is another way of perceiving the movement of the world. When I came to China I hoped to find a reservoir of thought and mysticism that would bring fresh youth to our West. I now have the impression that the reservoir is 'blocked'/emptied. The Chinese are primitive people (beneath their varnish of modernity or Confucianism); the Mongols are in gradual process of disappearance, and their lamas are coarse and dirty monks. The fact remains that in time gone by these people *saw something*, but that they allowed this light to be lost—and that we can rediscover it. I was positively moved by the serenity and majesty of a Buddha in Peking: we have no finer representation of the Divinity! I suspect these Orientals of being, essentially, innate adorers of material and nearby powers, and that they slumber embedded in that lower zone. Could we not enrich our spirit a little with the heavy sap circulating in their veins, while at the same time bringing them the wherewithal to make it live? Could we not try to complete ourselves by converting them? I haven't noticed that the missionaries have the faintest idea of this. But I am really rather too new to China to risk trying to teach them. I'm not saying that I won't write it when I get back. . . .

When I see the women round here, I often think of you—out of friendship first and foremost, but also in terms of 'feminism'. Chinese women are below anything. In these distant provinces, almost all of them have still got tiny feet, and it's pathetic to see them moving on

[1] Marguerite Teillard-Chambon (Claude Aragonnès), Teilhard's cousin.

their stumps (their legs are entirely atrophied) as on two
pegs: on the moral side they seem to be complete slaves,
as systematically crushed in their thinking faculties as in
their capacity to walk. The Mongol women are quite
another affair: they look you frankly in the eyes from beneath their coral-beaded diadems, and they ride on horse-
back like the men. I was told of a little girl of twelve who
can hobble horses, and of a Christian woman who goes
to Mass with three children on her mount. There you
have a fine race. What a pity that it is slowly dying out—
for lack of children (the eldest are consigned to the
lamaseries, and the custom is to adopt Chinese), and because, as everywhere, the herdsman is giving way to the
farmer (the Chinese). I remember running into a travelling family; they were obviously notabilities, to judge
by their embroideries, their jewels, and the red pointed
hats worn by the men: there were two men, one woman,
and a charming little boy of between twelve and fifteen,
and they were crossing the steppe to the swaying pace of
their camels. Well, it was the woman who led the way,
like a queen. I told myself that you would have liked to
see it.

I'm glad that the Le Roy lectures were as you say.[1]
Judging by your résumé, I feel that the separation of
spirit and matter as he admits it is too sharp. I incline to
admit that materiality is a *relative* thing (to a large extent):
for a being, that is material which is less spiritual than
itself (as the night is dark when you look *behind* the light
—but clear, ahead towards this light). Thus we have an
infinity of growing spiritualities. Man bears along with
him the world of beings inferior to God; sin lies in

[1] Édouard Le Roy, professor at the Collège de France, was Bergson's
deputy (1914-1920), and subsequently full professor (1921-1941). In
1922-1923 he gave the lectures which were to be included in *La Pensée
intuitive*, Paris, 1930.

plunging back into them; virtue, in carrying them forward.

Goodbye. I am sure your holidays will have done you good. No one can avoid momentary depressions: but you must never *doubt* the value of your effort to think better, in God: that's the great prayer.

Very faithfully,
Teilhard, s.j.

I'm going back to Tientsin in the first fortnight of October. I imagine you must have got the letter I wrote in June.

On the Yellow River,
October 3, 1923

Dear Mademoiselle,

I am writing to you from the middle of the Hwang-Ho, under a fairly comfortable tent pitched in the middle of a deep square boat which is whirling and drifting downstream rather like a tub. This skiff is taking us down from Ning-Sia to Pao-Teo (the railway terminus), and the journey is to take ten days if we don't get stranded or have bad weather. Our booty is piled up on board (sixty cases=three thousand kilos). There is no lack of the picturesque: to the left there slowly unfolds the high blue barrier of the Ala-Shan, frontier to the great empty spaces of Central Asia: to the right we have the outline of the grey and russet plateau of the Ordos which we have just been exploring. The banks are green with reeds, and wild geese frolic in hundreds in the muddy shallows. Over it all lies a slightly cold and misty sky such as you see in autumn on the high plateaux of Auvergne. Twenty years ago this would have enraptured me, but to-day it leaves me almost cold, for I have come to understand that neither the past nor space, as such, contain the solution to any mystery, and that all final and ultimate light lies in the future towards which we are leaning. . . .

All this is a prologue to telling you that three days ago, at Ning-Sia-Fu, I found your fine long letter of July 15 (by the way, I wrote to you around the middle of August: I hope the Chinese post has been reliable). Your letter gave me real joy, just like our talks at Neuilly, and what gave me even greater pleasure, besides the witness of your firm friendship, was the assurance in your letter that you were more and more set on the search for Divine Unity through all human effort. More than ever, you must refuse to let yourself be intimidated, or influenced, by what X or Y (or even Bremond) may say against intelligence as opposed to mysticism. Leave all those gentlemen to their little ideas. The truth is a question between you and God. No certitude, no human teaching, can go against the awareness you have of growing in light and strength in the direction that you have chosen. You're perfectly right in thinking that the best criterion of truth is 'the power of making ourselves coherent, *when put to the test.*' There is no trace of unsatisfactory pragmatism in this proposition, for we know that the truth when so recognised has a consistency and price outside our own success. I was amused and very pleased by Père Foch's advice to you. He's a man I only know by sight. But I hold him in esteem and believe him to be 'a friend' owing to several very excellent sentences on the universal Christ that he slipped into a little devotional book.[1] Did you know, by the way, that the second

[1] Germain Foch, s.j., *La Vie intérieure*, Paris-Lyon, Vitte, ch. 2, art. 3: 'The life of Jesus in us' (in the second edition of 1919, pp. 25-40). Mlle Zanta had made the acquaintance of Père Foch during the 1914-1918 war. He was an ardent disciple of Père Jean-Joseph Surin. Cf. R. de Sinéty, *Le Père Foch*, Toulouse, 1932.

series of Meditations by my friend Père Pierre Charles
(consult Marguerite for the reference) has been published[1]
and is full of things favourable to the ideas we hold dear?
Try to get hold of it. You could get many to read it.

I was telling you that I'm bringing back three thousand
kilos of precious material. As regards ideas, I don't know
exactly what I've picked up (the scientific work has been
pretty absorbing). I believe that at least I am leaving
Mongolia with a more and more passionate conviction
that the sole consistence of things (their only definitive
being, which upholds all the rest) is their organisation
in Christo. If you only knew how near I am to the certainty that, without this faith in a living *direction* in every
element and every effort, all would be but dust and ashes!
—and how more and more convinced I am that *all* can
be transformed and made divine in the Fire that envelops
us and only asks to come to rest on the soul of all we are
doing. . . . At Ning-Sia I had the satisfaction of running
into a missionary, a remarkable expert on Tibet to
whom (for the first time since I left France) I was able to
open my heart about these things. I think we understood
one another. He on his side (for the first time, too, since
I reached China) managed slightly to raise the veil of
coarse materialism beneath which I had lost all hope of
finding in China the faintest spark of true mysticism. He
showed me how the Chinese have been coarsened by
their Confucianism, which is a mere code of practical
ethics for the establishment of a comfortable social life,
without any appeal to a living ideal of any kind. But side
by side with this empiricism, suited for brutes, he assured
me that there existed (even now in the hearts of some

[1] Pierre Charles, s.j., *La prière de toutes les heures*, 2 vol., Charles
Beyaert, Bruges, 1923, Eng. revd. ed. in 1 vol., *Prayer for all Times*,
1948 London, Sands and Co. Handled in U.S.A. by Newman Press,
Westminster.

Chinese philosophers and lamas) the old Buddhist pre-occupation to sound the rhythm of the world, to establish a perspective of its countless evolutions, to await the supreme Buddha who is to redeem all things. Such assur-ances, coming from a man who has an intimate know-ledge of China, confirmed me in my old hope that we could perhaps learn from the mystics of the Far East how to make our religion more 'Buddhist' instead of being over-absorbed by ethics (that is to say too Con-fucianist), and at last discover a Christ who is not only *a model of good conduct* and of '*humanity*,' but the *super-human* Being who, for ever in formation in the heart of the world, possesses a being capable of bending all, and assimilating all, by vital domination.

I would like to write a certain number of things on these ideas. I don't know whether the writing-up of my journey will leave me much time. We'll see. . . . Mean-while I gather your novel is almost finished. Well done for the hard worker. And above all don't forget the Renaissance.

Goodbye. Your remembrance of me I faithfully return every day before God, when I commend to him those nearest to me 'in friendship and in thought.'

P. Teilhard, s.j.

Hautes Études, Race Course Road, Tientsin,
December 12, 1923

Dear Mademoiselle,

I am three letters behind you: the postcard from Le Lioran (which brought back so many happy memories), the letter from Chantilly (September 2), and finally the one from Neuilly (October 23). You are really very kind to write to me so often, and now and again by a long

letter to make up for our conversations at Neuilly—
which I often miss so much and from two points of view:
pleasantness and usefulness. You both forced me and
helped me to do a lot of thinking, while the lovely red
or golden sun sank down behind the plants on your balcony. I feel sure that such moments will come again.
Meanwhile, when the Tientsin evenings seem to me
rather cold and grey (to my heart rather than to my eyes
and skin), I think that one of the reasons why Our Lord
wanted me so far away at this moment was so as to
separate me, for a while, from those sweet things among
which I ran a risk of not relying uniquely enough on
him through and across all things (as I make it my profession to do). And I encourage myself to fast a little by
the very firm hope that, precisely because I am far away
and cut off, Our Lord will take my place beside friends
such as yourself—an exchange that could only be very
much to their advantage.

I was glad to see, in your last letter, that you were
remaining faithful to your own personal work, in spite
of the worries of teaching. Don't let Vittoria Colonna
sleep for too long (I am counting a lot on her), and don't
wait too long for the final documents on her before
filling her in. You're not a student at the École des
Chartes! Of course you have to have a serious historical
background for your study. But I feel that for you Vittoria Colonna ought to be first and foremost a symbol
through which you can say with passion what you want
to say about woman. Write it as Joergensen did his Saint
Francis or his Catherine of Siena[1] (or even Schuré his
'Joconde'[2]). Then you will have taken another important

---

[1] J. Joergensen, *Saint François d'Assise, sa vie et son oeuvre*, trans. from
the Danish by T. de Wyzewa, 1910, Eng. trs., 1912; *Sainte Catherine
de Sienne*, Paris, Beauchesne, 1920, Eng. trs., 1938.

[2] Here Père Teilhard is probably referring to the work of Édouard

step towards the influential position you would like to occupy so as to advance your 'Cause.' I understand your anxiety about not being up to the level of your task. This is one of the great human problems. You have to face this problem squarely, in God's truth and light—given that we live under this sun. Don't get lost in vain inner self-examination about your capacities and value. But tell yourself, categorically, that, for the success of the enormous work of Creation, God only needs one thing: that you should *do your best*. As soon as you give what you are capable of giving, you are united *in maximum measure* to the creative Act; you couldn't be a more useful servant. You must grasp this crucial point: only one thing matters in life (in order that it may be fulfilled) and that is to keep exactly to the place, willed by God, that is indicated at every moment by the equilibrium established between our effort (to succeed, and develop ourselves) and the resistance of things (which limit us). So long as we are in this place we are a faithful and supremely useful atom in the universe, truly annexed to the Body and Heart of Christ. And don't forget that if we lack power over our inspiration and intelligence, we have in addition the resource of intensifying our intention and our faith. The longer I plod on, the more I realise that on [that] side our power is prodigious. The weaker and less confident you feel in yourself, the more you need to strengthen in yourself the vision of the omnipresent Being to whom you have vowed your effort. The humblest effort, accomplished in this loving awareness of acting (physically) *in Christo*, has reverberations (and this is fundamental to the Christian's faith) on the real fibres of the world that no purely 'human' shock

---

Schuré: *Les prophètes de la Renaissance*: *Dante, Léonard de Vinci, Raphaël, Michel-Ange, Le Corrège*, Paris, Perrin, 1920.

could ever produce. All this amounts to saying: make good the deficiencies you feel by redoubling your inner life, your 'mystical vision'.

And then (I wonder if I've said it already) stop spending too much time in listening to what other people say, or in endless fresh probing into the foundations of your action. I feel, as you do, the metaphysical possibility that the universe could mark time and that the efforts of mankind could evaporate into nothingness. Like you, again, if I considered the question in isolation, I would be inclined to hesitate about what will remain of our consciousness after death. But there; I have seen and tested that there is no coherent life save in the overflowing faith in a universe whose every movement beckons us to a supreme Union. Since then I have had no other thought but to live and fulfil this faith. To satisfy it, I have a ferocious belief in progress of some kind, and I hold those who deny it as evil-doers and heretics. And, to attain tranquillity about the disturbing 'after life', I close my eyes in the arms of the greater-than-myself that draws me on. I don't think that the man who has always declared his trust in the energy that guides the world has anything to fear from it. In the beyond, we shall surely be something very new. But us it will certainly still be, but better.

I've little news of my life in Tientsin. Marguerite will have told you that I'm extending my stay in China by six months.[1] Giving her this pain has cost me more than anything else in this decision. But I wouldn't have deserved her friendship had I not done (for her) what seemed to me the best. (Take your share of all this, won't you?) The idea, as you must know, is for a second journey 'into Tartary' to be undertaken in the spring (which postpone

[1] Cf. *Letters from a Traveller*, 1923-1939, pp. 105-6; C. Cuénot p. 51.

my return until the summer). At first I was somewhat hesitant about going on this new expedition. But then M. Boule[1] (in a letter which arrived at the same time as yours), as well as my superiors, gave me formal encouragement to do so, so there's no question of holding back. The most trying part will be filling in the winter. But what with a few trips to Peking, the preparation of a few papers, and scraping a few fossils, the time will pass quickly. In one sense, this solitary life does me good, as it throws me back more uniquely on the Divine. But letters from you, too, will always do me good.

Faithfully,
P. Teilhard, s.j.

Write to me at the address written below. The Trans-Siberian leaves Paris on Thursday evenings.

Tientsin,
January 25, 1924

Dear Mademoiselle,

This letter will not be leaving for six days, but I don't want to delay my answer to your kind letter of December 28-31 which has just reached me. Thank you for all you tell me—it helps me to lead from afar a little of that warm Paris life of which I feel the lack quite a bit. I read your article on the Women's Working-Parties[2] with great

---

[1] Marcellin Boule, professor of Palaeontology at the Museum of Natural History in Paris, was the leading prehistorian and archaeologist in France at the time. (Tr..)

[2] *Équipes sociales féminines.* Mlle Foncin had started the women's *Équipes sociales* in 1922, and had asked for Mlle Zanta's collaboration. Mlle Zanta was immediately won over and played a very active part

interest. You are quite right in seeing these as a practical triumph for feminism: it is by imposing themselves in this way, much more than by discussing the legitimacy of their rights, that women will achieve their place in society. What you tell me, following Garric,[1] concerning the feeling for religion running through the mass of the people, usually viewed as the most uncivilised, is so much in the direction of my dearest wishes that my heart leapt for joy. Yes, steep yourself in that human material which, if a bit turbid, is very much alive. I am sure that the contact will act as a tonic on you. But don't forget your own important work, if earning your daily bread leaves you the time for it. Your real strength will always lie in the spiritual tension that you will succeed in maintaining within yourself by thought and by contact with God. I rather resented that first interruption in your letter which made you cut short the story of your young *agrégé* who wants to write a thesis on the Word. I'm so ignorant of modern history that I didn't realise that the seventeenth century (except for Surin and Lallemant) had any special understanding of the Universal Christ (weren't the men of that time too convinced that they had brought the world under control and too 'wise' to feel the need to dedicate themselves to the Whole?). Anyway, if your young friend has been able to find a historical way round the subject, that's marvellous. I'm very much afraid that if he wanted to tackle it head on through philosophy he'd

---

in the movement. She wrote regularly in the *Écho de Paris*, to which she had been introduced by the then editor, Henri Simon, and she wrote on this subject too, notably the front-page article on Tuesday, November 20, 1923: *Équipes sociales féminines*, signed 'Léontine Zanta, docteur-ès-lettres.'

[1] M. Robert Garric founded the *Équipes sociales* in 1919, and he himself had written them up in the *Écho de Paris* of August 12, 1923: *Les Équipes sociales et leurs oeuvres.*

soon have all the old guard of theologians on his track.
I'd be delighted to meet such a promising young man
when I get back. Do you know under whose influence
he's going to work?

Nothing very new as regards me. I'm occupying my
time as best I can while waiting for the month of April,
the time for me to set out on my second trip. This trip
is definite, in principle. In practice, I still have only a
vague idea of the direction I'll be taking. At the moment
there are brigands everywhere, beginning with the country I was travelling through last summer. Perhaps we
shall be thrown back on Eastern Mongolia (west of
Mukden). Throughout this month of January I've had
an opportunity of meeting a pretty large and varied
number of people—above all on the occasion of a geo-
olgical meeting in Peking: Chinese, Americans, English,
Russians, Swedes. . . . As in November (on a similar
occasion) I was struck by the cordiality that reigned over
this Babel from the start. There's no doubting that what
men lack, if they are to be good and happy, is a common
soul! The day before yesterday I dined very quietly with
the Chinese director of the Geological Survey,[1] and one
of his friends, also Chinese, the professor of Anthropology
at Tientsin University. Dr Ting, the director, is probably
the most open-minded and intelligent Chinese that I
know. In addition he is on friendly relations, and in
constant intellectual contact, with all the intellectual
'leaders' of young China to-day. While we were smoking
cigarettes or eating meat cut up into dice, rice, bêche-de-
mer soup and so on (fortunately I was provided with a
fork and spoon—not chopsticks) I boldly broached the
question of Chinese philosophy and the Chinese religious
temperament. The substance of Dr Ting's reply was as

[1] A Chinese, American and Swedish Organisation: in French, 'Service
géologique'.

follows: 'Like everyone on earth, the Chinese need a religion (that is, a justification of life). But for the moment they consider the problem too vast and complicated for there to be a solution in sight. Besides, at present, they are going through a period of reaction against their ancient superstitions. China is passing through an anti-religious phase like that of the French eighteenth century, and that suits her very well because by nature the Chinese are pragmatists and *agnostics*. At this moment they have no personal philosophy: their traditional thinking has been disrupted by political vicissitudes; and then they are still too much under the influence of American or European thinkers to try to open up new paths.' All this isn't very encouraging. Unquestionably the average Chinese is extremely earth-bound, and one may well ask oneself in what corner of his soul, or under what unexpected forms, the forces of religion and mysticism lie hidden in him. Even Dr Ting seemed to me to have envisaged the search for a religion in terms of a vast scientific enterprise, whereas the Absolute, as is only too clear, cannot '*be taken*' by force' but should $\left\{ \begin{array}{l} \text{manifest itself,} \\ \text{'give itself',} \end{array} \right.$ to the spirits that await it. What is certain is that if it is to attract the attention, and then the sympathy, of the Far Easterners, Christianity must present itself in a form (and it's what we want, isn't it?) which amplifies (not minimises!) the mystery, grandeur, interest and problems of the tangible universe.

I'm beginning to feel the need to get back to a milieu where I can discuss and preach these things. But all the same I think this year's long 'retreat' will have done me good. I have an impression that the earth, while retaining its prodigious power of communicating the Divine to us through all its being, is becoming paler and paler to me as regards its present and its past. It is the future that is fascinating, and I see it all ablaze with God springing up everywhere.

Courage! Yours,
P. Teilhard, s.j.

I can't remember how long it is since my last letter. Happy New Year, if I haven't already wished it. May Our Lord reveal himself to you in the smallest things, that's what I wish for you.

You must have been saddened by the death of poor Barrès!?[1]

Lin-hsi (Eastern Mongolia),
May 20, 1924

Dear Mademoiselle,

This is probably the last letter that I shall write to you from China. It is a rather late answer to yours of March 2 which reached me at the end of March, but as I left it behind in Tientsin I shall not be able to answer it very accurately. We set out on our second journey on April 3 and have now arrived at our destination, that is to say the Eastern border of the great Gobi plateau which we hope to penetrate at the end of the month, as soon as we have collected the Mongol wagons needed for that part of the journey. For nearly two months we have been travelling around on mule-back through a rocky, mountainous, cold and austere region, rather like the Cantal or Velay but totally denuded of trees and bushes. This state of things comes from the devastations caused by the Chinese colonists who are being punished for their lack of foresight by a tremendous erosion which is gradually carrying away all their land. Not far away, in Mongol country—or country sparsely colonised—

[1] Maurice Barrès had died suddenly on December 4, 1923.

the vegetation is richer. The brushwood is crammed with fine ring-necked pheasants. Nothing sensational in the way of finds so far; but plenty of solid work. We expect to go down from the Gobi towards the middle of July. I shall spend a month in Tientsin for the business of packing everything up. If all goes well I shall catch the first boat leaving Shanghai in September. So I should be in Paris towards the middle of October.

I get depressing news from Paris about the integrist movement.[1] My own resource shall be to limit my 'writings' to the domain of disputable facts. But you may be sure that no force on earth will make me modify the direction or intensity of all the influence of which I am capable. Only, let us ask Our Lord to help us to preserve this attitude without bitterness, by showing us that his activity can be incarnate even in the most disagreeable manoeuvres of various obtuse or pharisaical minds. My whole interior life is directed and confirmed more and more in union with God as found in 'all the inner and outer forces of this world.' But if this attitude is to be effective, *nothing* in these forces must be excluded; neither death, nor 'persecution' in the field of ideas. If we believe, everything can be transformed into Our Lord. I have probably told you already that the general formula of Christian life is expressed, for me, as follows: 'To communicate through fidelity with the world as consecrated by faith.' In my belief this proposition is exhaustive, and beyond attack.

You know with what great joy I am looking forward to seeing you in a few months' time. I am very sorry that the Collège de France affair is off.[2] But let yourself be

[1] i.e. of 'conservative' theologians (Tr.).

[2] There is no trace left of this 'affair' which would seem to concern Mlle Zanta. Perhaps it refers to some lectures that she was to have given at the Collège de France.

led by events, once they are stronger than you. You have great influence on many minds around you. Don't worry at finding this activity rather scattered, rather discontinuous. It isn't essential that we should understand our life absolutely and distinctly in order that it may be good and successful. Often an existence is fruitful on the side that one might be tempted to disdain.

Thanks, always, for your solid and beneficial friendship for Marguerite. Her letters give me plentiful evidence of what you mean to her. That, too, is a useful outcome of your life.

Have a good holiday, and faithfully yours,
P. Teilhard, s.j.

Tientsin,
August 28, 1926

Dear friend,

I've just found your excellent letter of June 27 on my return here. I, too, often dream that I am back in my customary place in your charming dovecote! My first journey wasn't the success I had hoped. Having set out towards the Tibet border, we had only got a third of the way when we were completely halted by war. We spent two months visiting a more accessible but less interesting region (Shansi). I hope my work was good: but it's all rather confused at the moment. Next month I intend to go and explore a rich fossil-bearing deposit two days' journey from Peking. Access to it has been made possible by a recent victory of the Mukden troops. It's impossible to foresee whether, by the spring, circumstances will allow me to reconsider a journey in the 'Far West' which I very much want to make. It's all a bit disconcerting. But after all nothing is absolutely priceless, absolutely essential—is it?—except the 'divine whim'. I'm delighted that your novel was treated with favour in the *Correspondant*,[1] and that Vittoria Colonna is going ahead. You know my views about this last. Try to be a solid historian of the past, but be even more an interpreter of the new aspirations. Vittoria Colonna should be a point of reference and a symbol for you. If you don't bring her to life exactly as she was, it doesn't matter. The main point is that she should bring you to life, and in some way be a cloak for you. As for me, I'm pretty absorbed in geology —as I should be. But I'm finding that it gives me the contact with the Real that I need so much, and I don't think my spirit is getting bogged down. I'm particularly struck, at the moment, by the period of waiting and expectation in which mankind finds itself as regards its most essential need—that of a Faith. As regards 'conversions', Christianity is visibly marking time. It is obviously not along current lines that God's Kingdom will be established—but by some rebirth, some 'revelation', which (once again in human history) will spread through the human mass like fire and water. That is what we must wish for and prepare for. I myself feel, as we have often said, that the spark will be struck by the conjunction that will sooner or later come about between Our Lord and the world within consciousnesses—the world becoming sacred and absolute in him at the term of the long creative effort. This is what should have been shouted to the Chicago crowds! This view of the immense simplicity and total divinisation of things seems to me more and more apparent, more and more within everyone's reach, more and more liberating. It draws off and synthesises, effortlessly, all that is good on every side. Say a prayer that when I get back from this journey I

[1] Mlle Zanta's novel, *La part du feu*, had just been published, and had been reviewed in the *Correspondant*.

may be better able to speak and make myself heard—
and also that Our Lord may provide me with the opportunity for speaking (if it isn't premature). One considera-
tion that helps me to be patient is this: that even if we
should not succeed during our lifetime in exteriorising
what we see—you, me and so many others—it would
already be a considerable achievement to have served
God as a testing ground for the marvellous alliance of
the love of heaven and the love of earth. Once the germ
has been inserted within a particle of the human mass,
it will inevitably spread through the whole body, without our knowing how. Everything lies in our being faithful in the hands, and under the influence, of God, and
this is what I ask for you every day.

My journey, alas, has not given me the chance to
savour the heady intoxication of the desert. I have been
mostly travelling round old China with its over-popu-
lated valleys and barren hills. All the roads are dirt tracks,
the pagodas are falling into ruin, the ancient steles are
sinking in the middle of the fields. And at the same time
one feels that the country's intellectual élite is rapidly
casting its skin. In a century the change will have happened. What will it give? A China capable of helping
the West in its Research, or merely an imitative China?
Who can say? . . .

I'm hoping for another letter soon. Write to me now
and again with news of *you* and news of Paris. You know
how much I look on you as a true friend.

Yours,
P. Teilhard, s.j.

Tientsin,
October 15, 1926

Dear friend,

I found your dear good letter of September 15 last
Sunday when I got back from a three weeks' trip north-
west of Peking—bringing with me a reasonable number
of fossils and geological observations. Knowing you as
I do, I wasn't sorry to hear that you had been rather
spoilt, from the material point of view, during your
holiday; and, at the same time, I liked the vigour with
which you pass judgment on those who allow themselves
to be sucked into and swallowed up by the comfortable
life. Doubtless it's hard to keep to the golden mean when
it comes to the possession and use of matter. But I persist
in my belief that it is better to try to transform it than to
run away from it. What, I feel, brings about the moral
ruin of the people you describe is not that they take hold
of matter, but that they take hold of it incompletely,
by easy little bits, instead of approaching it resolutely in
its total wealth, its sacred mystery, and its incomparable
majesty. The pleasure-seeker makes a misuse of the tangible because he breaks it up into such tiny pieces that he
sees himself as its master and possessor. Whereas if he
knew how to take an all-embracing look at the grandeur
of what he is profaning, he would—on the contrary—fall
on his knees. The fundamental evil that besets us (and I
think it is fundamental because it is the lack, the fore-
warning and the indication of the virtue or quality needed
for our progress at this moment) is our incapacity to see
the whole. Add this new way of seeing things to the
most disquieting tendencies of our time, and they would
be changed into magnificent virtues. I sometimes get
vague and undefined longings to gather a small group of

friends around me and—through all the admitted conventions—give the example of a life in which nothing
would count but the preoccupation with, and love for,
all the earth. What I'm saying must sound very pagan,
and far below the example of pure detachment formerly
given by a Saint Francis. But in last analysis (and of
course with no comparison of persons!) I wonder whether it might not, on the contrary, restart in its deepest
sense the movement of medieval conversions. Haven't
we often talked about this together? It looks as though
mankind will never regain its passion for God until God
is presented to it as the term of a movement that extends
our worship of the concrete Real (rather than tearing us
away from it). Oh, how tremendously powerful the Real
would be for lifting us out of our egoism if only we knew
how to see it in its prodigious greatness!

Yes, my dear friend, I rather envy you getting back
to the solid and exhilarating atmosphere of Paris. Surely
the spiritual layer in which the earth is enveloped has
greater tension there than anywhere else in the world. . . .
Yet I'm not unhappy in Tientsin. The calm to which I
have returned this lovely autumn, after seven months of
restlessness, seems exquisite to me, and I am beginning to
take advantage of it to pick up the threads of my medi-
tative work, side by side with my geological work. May
God preserve within me the deep taste, and the sort of
lucid ecstasy, that intoxicate me with the joy of Being—
a joy drunk in as though from an everlasting spring.
When I'm immersed in rocks and fossils, I sometimes feel
an indefinable bliss when I remember that I possess—in
a total, incorruptible and living Element—the supreme
Principle in which all subsists and comes to life. *Per
quem omnia semper bona creas, vivificas, sanctificas et praestas
nobis* . . . as we say at Mass. What science or philosophy
is comparable to the knowledge of that Reality—and

above all to the perception of it, even at the most modest and inchoate level! May God give that gift to you and me and preserve it within us. With the possession of that light and that fire one can go everywhere, enlightening oneself and nourishing oneself on everything.

My future plans are still very vague. But I think it would be better to wait till February or March to make a decision: a spring campaign if China calms down; return, if the chances of work disappear. Politically the situation is more disturbed than ever. At the moment the forces of Bolshevist tendency seem to be gaining the upper hand on the Yangtse. I'm beginning to think that their success would be the signal for the reorganisation of China—but at the expense of the Europeans. The Cantonese and Kuominchun hate the foreigner; but they seem to represent the only Chinese collectivity moved by high ideas, and capable of purging the country from the banditry of the military which is ruining it.

I'm glad you're going on writing. You must jealously reserve a place—if possible, in your very busy life—for your personal research and production. And tell me from time to time what is happening to you. Your letters are always a joy to me; and when I read them I imagine I'm sitting at the corner of the table near the lovely blue butterfly.

I pray for you every day.

Yours,
P. Teilhard, s.j.

Hautes Études, Race Course Road, Tientsin,
January 10, 1927

Dear friend,

I received your welcome letter dated November 14 shortly after New Year's Day—you forgot to address it 'via Siberia,' and that's why I appear to be answering it so late. Thank you for remembering me, and for evoking the friendly setting in which we've passed so many happy hours. I thought about it on the evening of December 31 while I was watching the last red sun of 1926 setting behind the marshy plain of Chihli. I remembered how at that same time in 1925 I was in your little haven wishing you a happy new year. And in my mind I began doing the same from afar—adding a good prayer to my wishes. Have a good year, my dear friend, may it be filled with God, with his light and his peace, and may we be granted the restorative vision of the mysterious Diaphany (I prefer that word to Epiphany) by which the universal Christ illumines the unique and higher substance of things, so as to act on us through them, and so as to draw us towards their common summit! The more I advance in life, the more I think that true wisdom, true 'philosophy,' consists in being able to discern—and then migrate to—this divine milieu, which is so mixed up with things, and yet so superior to them. Let's meet there, shall we? Naturally you know the ways that lead there, don't you?—otherwise we would never have met.

I'm so glad that you've remained loyal to Vittoria, and enthusiastic about her—and glad too that Providence has sent you a translator, thereby showing that with a little faith one can always rest on the events she brings to life 'for those who love.' In itself, your association with the *Écho de Paris* leaves me more doubtful[1]; but I feel you write your articles so spontaneously that I like them for the vital part of yourself that you put into them. But mind you see things from a broad angle! Here, around the Pacific, you couldn't believe how petty our little European disputes appear. I hope that we are gradually approaching a time when men will be capable of loving 'nothing but the earth.' Anything else is too small for us, you see. And even the earth, when we have encircled it with our union, will send us off to the love of what is greater still. I spent the whole month of December in Peking, busy seeing Americans, Australians, Dutchmen and so on, on their way back from the Pan-Pacific congress in Tokyo. You wouldn't believe how broadening this dive into an international élite is—on condition that one is also deeply rooted in one's own native milieu (which, for me, is obviously Paris!).

The stay in Peking I have just been talking about was an excellent opportunity for me to cement my friendships there as well as to visit the palaces, pagodas, etc., in the wake of the 'great men' whom I had come to meet. These visits didn't fill me with enthusiasm. What I like most in China is the geometry of the walls, the curve of the roofs, the multiple-storeyed towers, the poetry of the old trees teeming with crows, and the desolate outline of the mountains. The curios, the cloisonné enamels, the porcelains, the jades, fill me with horror. The only exception I make is for the jades of two thousand

[1] In 1927, as in the past, Mlle Zanta was writing for the *Écho de Paris*. Her articles included: *Plaidoyer de Diotime. A Mussolini* (January 31, 1927); *Variation sur un sermon* (March 13, 1927); *La France au visage de pierre* (May 18, 1927); *Un dialogue instructif* (June 6, 1927); *Contre le scandale d'une certaine vulgarisation* (July 26, 1927); *En marge de la Semaine Sociale de Nancy* (August 18, 1927); *Les responsables* (September 12, 1927); *Les voix du passé* (November 12, 1927); *La colline prédestinée* (December 24, 1927).

years before Christ, which have lines as pure as Egyptian jewels. One feels that at some given moment the Chinese became all twisted and complicated—just like that. With my friend and protector, M Lacroix,[1] I went on a geological excursion to Kalgan, in bitter weather and disorganised and dislocated trains. It was heroic, but highly successful. Kalgan, bordering on the Gobi, was incredibly picturesque in this season of cold and war. One could have been in the heart of Turkestan.

Here I'm living a regular and studious life. I'm identifying and preparing my fossils (at last I've got some fine material) and I'm writing a little spiritual treatise, *Le Milieu Divin* (!!) which I hope will be orthodox. Intellectually (and almost mystically, at certain junctures) I'm gradually feeling the axis of my scientific tastes and preoccupations moving from the material or living layers of the earth towards the thinking layer—which on our planet is composed of mankind. It is in that human zone, it seems to me, that geology and palaeontology have their real extensions; and it's there that I believe I can perceive the essence of what drew me towards these other sciences. When—with the help of studying rocks and old bones—you have once grasped the order of magnitude and the organic stage of the human milieu in which we are immersed, I can assure you that one has a magnificent object of study. We still seem strangely indifferent before this object, as our ancestors were before mountains. But in a century or two from now, mankind will have become a classical subject of studies, the higher goal of 'Natural History'; and I suppose that there will then be agreement on this point: that the first physical, organic condition of mankind's balance and progress lies in belief

[1] M Alfred Lacroix, permanent secretary of the Academy of Sciences, who died in 1948.

in God—faith in a $\begin{Bmatrix} \text{definite} \\ \text{absolute} \end{Bmatrix}$ End of the movement that is carrying us along.

Send me your news from time to time, and news of friends; and convey all my friendliest greetings to Garric, whom I haven't forgotten. I know he's doing good work.

I expect to stay in Tientsin until April. Then I'll try to go off on another trip. Back in Paris in the autumn at the latest I should think.

All yours, dear friend,
P. Teilhard, s.j.

Remember me to your niece and her little family.

Tientsin,
May 7, 1927

Dear friend,

I haven't yet answered your letter of March 6. In fact it's so long ago since I last wrote to you that I don't know exactly what point I had reached. Thanks, in any case, for giving me your news from time to time, and news of our world in Paris. I need it, both for my heart and mind.

Briefly, my position is as follows. In general terms, it seems to be definite that I'll be returning to Paris in the autumn, and that after a few months, and when I've got a publication ready, I'll be coming back for a further period in China where the National Geological Survey holds out interesting offers of work. To go into more detail, I shall probably be setting out next week on a trip to the north-west of here and lasting only two or three months—an unambitious journey in country of only mediocre interest but where at least I shall be able to collect some new pieces of evidence. I feel a real need of getting out into the wide open spaces. During my next stay in China my life will be altogether more organised, more taken up with regular occupations. As things are, I have finished my study on the material collected in 1925-1926 and feel thoroughly 'at a loose end.' I need some active life. I'm operating rather in a vacuum—except during my visits to Peking (I've made three, I think, since my last letter).

As you will know, at the end of March we went through a critical moment here in China. Revolution was on the point of breaking out in Peking, Tientsin, Harbin and elsewhere. Had it not been for the dissension of the Cantonese and the raid made by Chang-Tso-lin on the Russian legation in Peking, there would have been real trouble. As things stand, it appears that the Communists have lost the game in the Far East. But the evolution of people's minds has happily not stopped. I hope that the conservative reaction won't be too brutal nor last too long—though people are beginning to talk of Chinese Fascism! Here, you know, dictators are pretty tough: in the past weeks eighteen students have been executed in Tientsin! . . . It must be admitted that the South Chinese played their hand stupidly. But for all that my sympathies are somehow with them, and I hope that their 'humanitarian' spirit will come out on top. One feels it everywhere already. I find it more and more difficult to form any exact idea as to what sort of greatness or renewal we should expect from the New China. Sometimes I feel pessimistic. What seems clear to me is that we must look with favour on the 'birth' of a new human group that nothing can prevent. Later we shall see what can be done with the baby. Apart from some disagreeable symptoms (such as a narrow hatred of foreigners), I have been fortunate enough to come across all sorts of re-assuring indications in the past three months as to the possibility of frank spiritual collaboration between East and West. Look: we just can't breathe in our different compartments, our closed categories. Without destroying our more limited organisms, we must fuse them together, synthesise them: man, nothing but man, nothing less than man as the context of our ambitions and organisations. Why in the world do we have to repeat this to Catholics? The fact is, one sometimes gets the impression that our little churches hide the earth from us. I've just remembered a thought I first had over ten years ago. There are some who want to identify Christian orthodoxy with 'integrism,' that is to say with respect for the tiniest wheels of a little microcosm constructed centuries ago. In reality, the true Christian ideal is 'integralism,' namely the extension of the Christian directives to all the resources contained in the world. Integralism or integrism, dogma-as-axis or dogma-as-framework, there we have the struggle that has been going on in the Church for more than a century. Integrism is simple and convenient, both for the faithful and the authorities. But it implicitly excludes from God's Kingdom (or denies, on principle) the huge potentialities whirling around us in social and moral questions, in philosophy, science, etc. That is why I have declared war on it to the death. . . . I don't quite know how I'll set about waging this war, now that my possibilities of outside action have become more and more restricted. But Our Lord will help me, if he is with me. Sometimes I think that the best way of making an attitude triumph is to live it as faithfully as possible. Let's do that together, shall we?

I am so glad to know, through your letters, that your activity continues. You're quite right to throw yourself headlong into faith, that is into a complete surrender to the world as animated by God: all that is asked of us is to try, ceaselessly, to climb upwards towards more breadth and more light, without letting go of these two threads: loyalty towards ourselves, and attachment to the Church. Pray that I may never break either of them. I ask the same for you. Please remember me warmly to Garric, and for you my deep friendship.

P. Teilhard, s.j.

To return to the (deserved) setback of the Communists in the Far East, my feeling is that this defeat of an effort at 'internationalisation *through hatred*' should be the signal for the awakening of an effort (a vigorous and constructive one) at internationalisation through sympathy and mutual assistance. What distresses me is to see Communism resisted by Fascism, that is to say the brutal and retrogressive negation of what has been dimly foreseen and desired by many *good* elements in the Communist *awakening*. 'Nothing but Man,' once again. . . .

Le Chambon,[1]
August 22, 1928

Dear friend,

I found your very kind letter of Saturday waiting for me when I got back from Montsalvy last night. It touched me very much—without telling me anything entirely new. For long I've felt you to be my true friend; and a restful friend, owing to being so totally trustworthy and so truly on the same plane (as we say). We must count ever increasingly on God to make this generous force serve some ever nobler purpose. Don't be afraid of the 'evil forces' you feel prowling around your old castle. Such phantoms vanish with the first rays of faith, in proportion to our faith in the (not first, but) final goodness and value of things. For myself I have no other per-

[1] Marguerite Teillard's country home, cf. above p. 17.

sonal guide-line of conduct than this: 'to believe in the Spirit,'—in the Spirit, the supreme value and criterion of things; in the Spirit, the living and loving organiser of the world. Have trust in the world as given life by Our Lord and the world will save you. I think that, as in the Gospel, the moving waters bear us up inasmuch as we dare walk upon them, provided we are going in God's direction and in God's love. Walk straight, un-hesitatingly, and you will see that the mist will disperse, even from one step to the next. But, naturally, pray that God may help you. Throughout the whole of life there is a sort of struggle between ourselves and things: either they will dissolve us into them, or else we will absorb and assimilate them. Victory goes to the stronger, that is to the more one, that is to the more spiritual, that is, finally, to the more united with God. In fact, I hope your shadows have already dispersed; and that you'll manage to spend your days on the Loire happily and profitably.[1]

. . . [2] What a strange mad force the heart is; nowhere else does life seem so rich, so new-born, and so disturbing. How are we to transfigure this without impoverishing it? That's the whole secret of creation.—We have spent nearly all our time touring by car: in Aubrac, in the Aveyron; and we even came back through Salers,[3] where I missed you. . . .

Here everything seems to be going normally. I expect to go to the Ariège[4] at the beginning of next week.

All yours,
P. Teilhard, s.j.

[1] At the Manoir de la Voulte, with Mme de Polignac, on the banks of the Loire.

[2] Here a line in the manuscript has been omitted.

[3] Mlle Zanta was having a few days' rest at Salers, in the Cantal.

[4] To Montesquiou-Avantès, near Saint-Girons. Cf. the following letter.

Les Espas, Montesquiou-Avantès, par St-Girons, Ariège,
September 1, 1928

Dear friend,

I haven't yet thanked you for your kind postcard 'from
Salers' which reached me when I was still at Le Chambon.
I was delighted to get the proof that your holy optimism
had finally pierced the clouds that were befogging you.
The truth, I think, is that to conquer the world there is
no better means (and anyway it's in the Gospel) than to
believe vigorously that the universe and its powers are
good, provided we approach them laboriously and faithfully in the direction in which things become better and
more one. The mistake lies in imagining that all is naturally, initially, statistically good. Truth lies in seeing that
everything gives way in the direction, and under the influence, of beauty and goodness. That is the inner face
of evolution. . . .

I got here on Tuesday, in time to have 48 hours with
Breuil and benefit by his wise advice. Now I'm almost
alone, in the wide calm, among little chalky hills, pierced
by thousands of caves peopled by a prehistoric world;
looking towards the Pyrenees, high crests of naked granite
mark the Spanish frontier, preceded by great wooded
ridges like the Bois du Roi. I'm profiting by this isolated
retreat to set down a few ideas that will go, perhaps, into
Scientia.[1] I have no clear idea as to what this piece of
writing is worth. In any case, I'll be staying here until it's
finished. And then I'll be setting out for Paris (5, rue du
Regard) where I expect to arrive around the 10th. Other-

[1] 'The Phenomenon of Man.' Cf. the next letter. This was the title
of an article published in *La Revue des Questions Scientifiques*, November,
1930; it appears in *Vision of the Past*, London, Collins, and New York,
Harper & Row, 1966, pp. 161-74.

wise, nothing new. My review of Le Roy, signed Max
Bégouën, was given prominence in *La Vie Catholique* of
August 17.[1] A stone at de Sinéty. . . .[2]

Goodbye; and may Our Lord be with us.

My respects to the Comtesse.[3]

Yours,

P. Teilhard, s.j.

5, rue du Regard, Paris, VI,
September 28, 1928

Very dear friend,

I haven't yet answered your letter of September 9
which missed me in the Ariège and caught up with me
here where I've been since the 12th. I would have liked
to have sent you my greetings sooner. But from the very
first moment I got caught up in the turmoil of Paris, even
of an almost empty Paris. But all the same I'd like to send
you a few friendly lines, as well as news, before your
return to Neuilly.

There isn't really much in the way of news. Since I got
back here I've taken up work again on a memorandum
that I'd like to leave in a fairly finished state when I go.
The work has made good progress. But I have to reckon
with a photographer and the sun, neither of which is
exactly reliable. Also I have to give time to preparing for
my departure, which will probably be very early in
November. I still don't know (and have no means of

---

[1] *La pensée dans la science*, under the pseudonym of Max Bégouën
(a close friend of Teilhard's. Tr.), appeared in *La Vie Catholique en
France et à l'Étranger* (5th year, no. 203) on Saturday August 18, p. 5.
It was devoted to Édouard Le Roy's work, *L'exigence idéaliste et le
fait de l'évolution* (Paris, 1927).

[2] Two manuscript lines have been omitted.

[3] Comtesse Melchior de Polignac.

knowing) how long this new absence will last. But so far as the intentions of my Order are concerned, I'm leaving on the same conditions as formerly, that is to say for a limited period. The rest will depend on the state of Chinese politics, as well as on my eventual findings.

As regards people in Paris, I saw Marguerite for two days—she had to go back to la Voulte this morning. I've also seen Le Roy who arrived the other day. His second volume (on Man) should be out almost immediately.[1] What a pity that his book isn't twice as short and twice as tersely written! As for me, I've written (as I've already told you, I think) a dozen pages on 'The Phenomenon of Man'; I've just sent them off to Louvain for 'revision.' I'd like to see them appearing in the review *Scientia*. But I've no precise idea what sort of reaction reading them will have on people unfamiliar with the ideas I'm putting forward; I'm wondering if it won't all seem rather mad.

For the rest, I am still convinced that nothing is of any value, or can be constructed, save through, and in, faith in the spirit. But at the same time I am aware how difficult it is to lead certain intelligences and certain sensibilities to this point of view. But this difficulty should have no other effect on us but to urge us forward to a greater faith—don't you agree?

I hope you're spending tranquil and profitable hours among the vines of the Gironde.[2] I know you won't fail to let me know when you get back to Neuilly.

All yours,
P. Teilhard, s.j.

[1] Édouard Le Roy, *Les origines humaines et l'évolution de l'intelligence.* Boivin, Paris, 1928.

[2] Mlle Zanta was staying with friends in the Gironde.

Obok,
January 24, 1929

Very dear friend,

I'm very cross with myself for not having answered before now your very kind letter of November 24. I haven't yet even wished you a happy new year. Though as January 1 drew near, my memory went back to those happy gatherings at which we have celebrated the last days of December whenever I've been in France since 1920. Never doubt my faithful and ever-growing friendship.

I am due to sail again in about twelve days' time. My trip to Somaliland and Ethiopia is finishing, as it started, in dear old Obok.[1] Imagine a large old house situated between the blue or phosphorescent-green sea which beats against our walls, and an immense stretch of golden desert bordered to the west by tall purple mountain tops. Round this dwelling, place twenty or so Dankali straw huts, and visualise an interior decoration which—apart from a few hangings put up in the past by Madame de Monfreid—suggests a fisherman's cabin or the deck of a ship. Then imagine me, your humble servant, in espadrilles, khaki trousers, and short-sleeved shirt. That's the way it is—and it's symbolic of the existence I've been leading for nearly three months. Fortune sometimes has its revenges. . . .

In a word, all goes well. Physically, I'm nearly as sunburnt as de Monfreid himself. Scientifically, I've made some useful discoveries in geology and Prehistory. As for morale, after a period of eclipse in the turmoil

[1] Père Teilhard spent two months (end of November 1928 to beginning of February 1929) on the French Somali coast as the guest of Henri de Monfreid. Cf. *Letters from a Traveller*, pp. 144-50.

of material things, I feel I'm in pretty good shape; which means that I have a fairly intense perception of 'the taste for Being'. Once again, the great animating Power, to which it is so good to entrust ourselves, seems—in a motherly way—to have brought the inner and outer forces of the world into harmony around me. It's certainly an encouragement to go on, don't you think?

I won't go into great detail about my comings and goings in this region. It would take rather long, and as you don't know the country you wouldn't find my descriptions very interesting. All I need say is that I've passed through or stayed in a great variety of regions: the burnt-up deserts of the coast, the Afar bush still inhabited by great antelopes, the high plateau of the Harar (well over 6,000 feet) where it was almost cold at night, over millet fields and great lush euphorbia like candelabra, the valley of the Errer (south of the town of Harar) where I stayed a month among coffee shrubs, banana trees, papaw trees, parrots, toucans and monkeys, facing the great bush of the South, still very mysterious. All this new country as I saw it with my friend de Monfreid (we get on better and better, he and I, as regards fundamental appreciation of the universe and simplicity of external life) immediately seemed home from home to me, and I can't help wondering whether I won't end up by coming back here. It's nearer than China, after all. (Yet oddly enough it doesn't stop me from feeling a sort of homesickness for Mongolia.)

When I go down into the depths of myself (for three months, I must confess, I have made do with interior prayer and the 'Mass on the World,' and, of course, my breviary; but that doesn't worry me, you know—rather, it *rests* me)—well, when I recollect myself a bit, I notice that my thought continues to go on its way and organise itself in silence. In a rather odd way the 'Spirit' has now become an entirely real thing for me, the only real thing, not as the result of a sort of 'metaphysicisation' (!?) of matter, but as the result of a 'physicisation' of the Spirit. I see all the attributes that science has accumulated round matter in the last 150 years, whether as regards energy or history, transposing themselves and passing over onto Spirit. As I see things, the universe, through all its experimental organisation (and the extensions of this) is not descending towards the homogeneous and the most probable: its equilibrium lies in falling laboriously (if the phrase may be permitted) onto the personal, the differentiated, the conscious. 'Consciousness' (that is to say the tension of union and desire) has in my eyes become the 'fundamental element,' the very stuff of the real, the veritable 'ether'; and the current 'towards greater consciousness' should, it seems to me, displace physically the current of 'Entropy' in its dignity as current expressing 'the universal drift.' All present-day physics of matter is merely the study of a *wave motion*. (Bergson came very near to saying that, but didn't quite say it, I think: spirit and matter, for him, are two powers that are inverse yet of almost equal cosmic value—am I not right?) The fact remains that, in my eyes, souls, and the Soul of souls, are taking on more and more the form of consistent and real things. To dissolve a soul seems to me, in all sincerity, infinitely more difficult than to split an atom. Doubtless with survival after death, the soul is introduced into organisations of which we can only speak by analogy—as with divine qualities; but the more the soul is centred, the more stable it is, with the stability of the universe itself. I've been asking myself whether these views are not a mere accommodation I have made so as to save by artifice a datum imposed on me by the Christian Faith. But in all truth I don't think so. To be sure, perhaps I would never have arrived at this view of things but for my religious education. Moreover it is of great price to feel oneself in fundamental conformity with the huge philosophico-moral current whose axis is Christianity. But, this having been said, it seems to me nonetheless that if, now, all these solid props were to crumble, I could not see things otherwise than I do.

I do so hope that Vittoria Colonna is soon to make her second entry into the world, and that all goes well with you, physically, materially and morally. Let me know, whenever you have time. I'm setting out from Jibuti on February 4 and shall reach Tientsin at the beginning of March. If you write to me, don't forget to put 'via Siberia.'

All yours, my friend, *in Christo*,

P. Teilhard, s.j.

Every warm wish to Donnay[1]—and to the little family.

Continue, if you can, to put yourself, every day in the morning, in contact and in conformity with the One and Only Activator and the One Thing Needful! . . . It's the great fount of life.

---

[1] Maurice Donnay had frequented Mlle Zanta's salon ever since he had first called on her to gather information for his play, *Les éclaireuses*. In an article of October 1, 1917 (*Le déjeuner* in the *Revue des Deux Mondes*, 1917, vol. 5, pp. 481-511), Donnay—known familiarly as 'Uncle Maurice' in the Avenue de Madrid—described the 'radiant welcome' he received from 'Mlle Lanéo,' the 'doctoress,' the 'Christian and metaphysician.' 'With her extreme sensitiveness, her ardent charity, her stoical will; with her face and still young complexion beneath her white hair, with her eyes at times laughing, at times serious, with her hands and tapering fingers indicative of spirituality, she was the link between true reality—to use her language—and the reality of appearances.' (*op. cit.*, p. 510.)

Peking,
April 15, 1929

Very dear friend,

I haven't yet answered your long letter of March 15
(always write to me *via Siberia*), and yet I was infinitely
touched by it. I think in my whole life I shall never know
a joy so sweet as that of feeling my thoughts, which are
the best part of me, passing into the heart and thought of
friends such as yourself. Thank you for having given
me this happiness. And then, of course, you mustn't stop
at me: let us try to press forward into the '*Terra nova*' of
the spiritualisation of matter. It occurred to me that one
could write an essay entitled: 'The Third Spirit'—by
which I mean the Spirit of the divinisation of the world,
as opposed to what is called 'The Spirit of God,' and 'The
Spirit of the world,' an over-simple alternative. It is
approximately the subtitle that I put long ago (1916) on
my first paper of any note: 'There is a communion with
God, and a communion with earth,—and a communion with God through earth.'[1] As regards this,
I suppose that it is not without reason that you find
Bergson's interpretation of matter inadequate. This in-
adequacy must derive from the fact that, though a philosopher, he was too anxious to keep to a mere recording
of appearances, without attempting an explanation of
the whole. As for me (I may have already written this
to you in January) I've reached the point of being unable
to imagine the world, even physically, other than in
the form of a huge movement of spirit. I'm thinking of

[1] This 'first paper of any note' was *La Vie cosmique*, since published
in Teilhard de Chardin's *Écrits du temps de la guerre*, 1916-1919, Paris,
Grasset, 1965, pp. 1-61; Eng. trs. *Writings in Time of War*, London,
Collins and New York, Harper & Row, 1968, pp. 14-71.

writing a short piece entitled: 'The Physics (not the Metaphysics!) of the Spirit.'

Meanwhile, since Sunday last, I've been putting together a fairly elementary, but substantial, article on: 'What should we think of Transformism?' I was urged to do so for a Bulletin widely read among the missionaries in China—with a view to giving them some guidance in the use of Chinese school handbooks. If my article gets through the censorship I shall send it to you, and I may send it to the *Revue Pratique d'Apologétique* (of the Institut Catholique of Paris).[1]

As you see, I'm writing to you from Peking, where I've been spending three of the six weeks that I've now been in China. This is because the natural development of my contacts—and also of Chinese affairs—have brought me into closer and closer collaboration with the Chinese National Geological Survey. It's even possible that at the end of May I may be setting out on a journey (two or three months) with a Chinese attached to the Survey, and not with my friend Licent. This may herald a pretty serious change in my life. I'm not too sure where 'the thread of my life' is leading me. I like Peking a lot—it reminds me of Paris (though with too many friends missing. . . .). It suits me because I meet so many active and original people in all walks of life, and in the relative isolation in which we all find ourselves we naturally exchange ideas with great frankness and intimacy. And then the setting pleases me, because of its almost cynical serenity. The world and China can rock from one end to the other: while Peking remains unshakable under its blue sky, among its white flowers, and in the midst

[1] This article, entitled *Que faut-il penser du transformisme?* appeared in the *Dossiers de la Commission synodale*, Peking, vol. 2, June-July 1929, pp. 462-9, and, the following year, in the *Revue des questions scientifiques*, January, 1930, 4th series, vol. 17, no. 1, pp. 89-99. It is included in Teilhard's *Vision of the Past*, pp. 151-60.

of its prodigious dust. Tientsin suits me too: but there the life is one of calm retreat, of thought and prayer and quiet regularity. The truth is that after six months of travel I would quite welcome a little calm; but I mustn't think of that before the autumn.

In a word, all goes well. This winter I went through a rather bad crisis of anti-ecclesiasticism, not to say anti-Christianity. But now this outburst has melted away into a broader and more peaceful outlook. Given that my only rule of appreciation and practice is tending more and more to become, 'Believe in the spirit,' it would indeed be unjust to see the Church as the one thing in the world that lacked it. I incline to believe that the source of most of our weaknesses is to be found in the fact that we do not 'believe' to the very end, nor on a wide enough scale: to stop believing a second too early, or to believe in an inadequate object, can be enough to ruin the whole edifice we are building.

Write to me from time to time; it does me good, both in heart and spirit. And good luck for Vittoria and Saint Odile.[1]

All yours,
P. Teilhard, s.j.

Please remember me to M. Donnay.
Every sort of wish to the little family.

[1] Besides her study of Vittoria Colonna, Mlle Zanta was engaged on a work that was to come out in 1931: *Sainte-Odile*, 'Les pèlerinages' series, Paris, Flammarion. Cf. the letter below dated December 14, 1929.

From an inn in the depths of the Shansi,
August 23, 1929

Very dear friend,

Persistent rain, the terror of the traveller on mule-back, is holding me up in an unmentionable little inn in the Shansi. The clouds are slowly emptying themselves over the conical hills of yellow earth (loess) all around us, positively inundating the almost vertically sloped fields of millet and sorghum. So what better can I do than transform this universal boredom of things into a delightful if distant chat with you? I have had so little leisure for this in the last three months or more; and I have to answer your so kind letter of Whit Monday which reached me in Tientsin just before my last departure.

Externally, my situation and occupations have been as follows: After spending the month of May mostly with my colleague, Père Licent, in Manchuria (I went along the Trans-Siberian railway right as far as the Siberian frontier—9 days from Paris . . .), I set out again, (towards mid-June) on a second and more serious journey, this time as 'honorary adviser' to the Chinese Geological Survey, with papers from the Nanking government, and in the company of a Chinese geologist.[1] We assembled a little caravan of six mules; and for the last two months we've been wandering over the Shansi mountains and the southern sands of the Ordos. We are now on our way back to Peking by a rather roundabout route. I expect to be in Tientsin towards the end of September. The scientific results have been excellent. It was

[1] C.C. Young, a young Chinese geologist who was assistant director of the Cenozoic Research Laboratory to which Père Teilhard had just been attached. Cf. George B. Barbour. *In the Field with Teilhard de Chardin*, New York, Herder & Herder, 1965.

not without some misgivings that I decided in April to 'go over to the Chinese.' But I'm now congratulating myself. And I hope that this success will make it easier for my superiors in Europe to swallow the pill—I think they've had the impression that I was making decisions rather as if I was a law unto myself. Yet how can I consult them, from this distance? Providence, which is watching over me in such a patient and touching way, willed that my friend, the rector in Tientsin[1] (who is wholly on my side), should go to Europe just this last month. I feel sure that he will have straightened everything out, if this was necessary. With all this, what is my outlook for the future? I have no very clear idea. I can see a lot of laboratory work ahead of me this coming winter in Tientsin and Peking and doubtless another journey in the spring of 1930. After that I'd very much like to return and use France as my base. But this is all very uncertain. Am I, by the sheer force of things, moving towards settling in China with frequent visits to Europe? . . . Sometimes I wonder. And yet I am not yet prepared to abandon my dream of some stable activity in Paris. In last analysis everything depends on how my *official* relations with Rome develop; and I'm very much afraid that I'll never manage to regain a 'clean slate' in that quarter.

I underlined the word 'official' because, on the *interior* and deeper side, I feel that you need have no worries about me. I feel that in this last period I have finally 'emerged' morally from my Order, in the sense that I now have the impression that I can dominate it and judge it (without the faintest suggestion of conceited superiority, I think; but simply because I have in some way become adult, or attained my majority). But at the same

[1] Père Teilhard's superior was Père Auguste Bernard, rector of the Hautes Études in Tientsin from July 3, 1925, to June 27, 1931, at which date he was replaced by Père René Charvet.

time, though for reasons rather different from those of my youth, I feel myself deeply and heartily attached to it (as to my natural point of insertion in the universe); and unless (which is highly improbable) I found myself forced into some intellectual dishonesty, I am determined to remain faithful to it whatever the cost. This means that, with the help of God and my friends, I hope I have weathered last year's storm with no broken bones—it unquestionably marked a turning-point in my intellectual and emotional life. Without any failure of inner logic, I think I have just about integrated, into a proper Christian attitude, many elements (still but little Christianised) which had gradually revealed themselves to me as the essential factors of my life. In other words I am at peace, truly at peace, with the Church as with God.

You may perhaps say that it is easy enough to preserve such peace when one is travelling about, as I am, beyond the reach of all painful ecclesiastical friction. That may well be. Meanwhile I'm taking advantage of the situation. In the last two months I have again started to live that life (familiar to me since the war) in which my most substantial spiritual nourishment (with a real Mass at infrequent intervals) lies in the mental Mass 'on the world' that I have often spoken to you about and at which you are always present. I am ceaselessly deepening and working over that Mass. If I get time this autumn I'll set it down in its nth form. I rather feel it is now reaching whatever degree of perfection I'm capable of giving it.

I would like to be with you, in 'the' armchair, so as to explain yet another thing to you. I mean the extraordinary development that the notion or value of the 'person' has taken on in my intellectual constructions. After spending some ten years over the very simple reversal of views on the world which consists in searching for the consistence of the universe, that is to say of evolution, ahead, in Spirit (and not behind, in matter), I now perceive this other elementary truth, namely that Spirit could never reach fulfilment save in personality (or hyper-personality). And thus the fundamental problem of action ('How to $\begin{Bmatrix} \text{save} \\ \text{justify} \end{Bmatrix}$ the value of and taste for progress in the eyes of reflective, hominised consciousness?') comes down to that of personalisation ('How to save the individual human personality, and how to conceive a personality of the universe?'). From this fact I find myself back at giving primacy (in the universe) to the immortal soul and to the risen Christ; that is to say I have rediscovered the exact Christian perspective, but *grafted* (as it should be) onto a universal and evolutive perspective. Thenceforth the 'Person' is no longer a sort of plural and artificial absolute. It is the bound-up product of an immense labour of concentration. Evolution=spiritualisation=personalisation. And, to come back to my 'Mass,' the great significance of the Chalice (the great value of *divinised* suffering) lies in expressing the twofold preliminary rupture required for supreme unification (personalisation): rupture (as it were) in the Creator, so as to admit creation in Him; and rupture in the personalities of creatures so as to pass into God. In a similar way, if the Universe needs, *by the very structure of Being*, to fulfil itself in 'person,' there must be some *Revelation* of the Centre-Person to the 'elementary-persons'; as no one can penetrate to the core of the Centre save the Centre itself. Only Christ, *who is conscious of his situation*, can say of the universal labour: '*Hoc est Corpus meum.*' And so on.

During the last fortnight my thoughts have often gone back to August of last year: Le Lioran, Le Puy Mary, Salers. Would we could always, my dear friend, climb the summits with each other's support! Those were delightful days. Where are you on holiday now, I wonder? and what is happening in poor old Le Chambon? My last news from Europe dates back to the beginning of June. I've heard nothing more about Cécile[1] or Marguerite, nor from my family for that matter where a difficult birth was expected in July; and I shan't hear anything for a month. These long silences are one of the great drawbacks to my sort of travelling. . . .[2]

And, as for me here, I often think that the world, not only in its physical but also in its moral aspect, is infinitely vaster and more *unexplored* than comfortable moralists, so sure of the geometry of their principles, suppose.

Write to me now and again, dear friend. And rest assured of my great attachment to you in Christ. Remember me with all friendship and respect to Donnay.

Yours,
P. Teilhard, s.j.

The National Geological Survey of China,
December 14, 1929

Very dear friend,

I've got very late for sending you my wishes for 1930. But we are too sure of one another, now, for you to doubt that at this time of year my daily remembrance of you, before God, is warmer and more pressing. Yes, dear friend, whatever happens I wish you a good and fruitful year in the great pacifying intensity of the divine Omnipresence. Would I be telling you anything new if I said how much your steadfast friendship becomes more

[1] Cécile Teillard-Chambon, Père Teilhard's cousin and younger sister of Marguerite.

[2] Seven lines of manuscript have been omitted.

precious to me every year because in it I find un-
alloyed strength? Keep it for me.

I got your good long letter of October 13 towards
the middle of November—and found it full of heartfelt
wisdom. I was delighted to hear that you had written a
book about *Sainte-Odile*[1] (I spent a few hours at the
convent when on a geological expedition in September
1925). But I'd also like to know that your tiredness is
a thing of the past. I'm hoping for a line from you
towards the end of January.

What can I tell you about myself? Since I got back
from my last trip, I've spent nearly all my time at the
Geological Survey in Peking. I've only spent three weeks
in Tientsin. I shan't be able to continue like this all winter
because of my colleague Licent's museum, to which I
have to devote some care; and besides I need the calm
of Tientsin. But my activities with the Chinese are certainly developing—there is plenty of interesting work,
and I have the satisfaction of collaborating in an important
organisation. My Order (except perhaps Licent, as is
only to be expected) views this situation with a favourable
eye. All the same I'd like to escape to France, at least for
a few months, towards the end of 1930. But this idea
hasn't yet been put up to the authorities on whom I
depend. All in all, I've never been so calm as now. I have
an ever accentuated impression of 'inner escape' away
from all the apparently most constricting aspects of outward organisation (an impression of which I probably told
you in my last letter): so that among examples of
narrowness against which I used to be so in revolt, I
now have a feeling that 'they no longer touch me.' No
question of pride, I feel, nor contempt—and equally no
holiness: but simply the fading-away of all that is seen as
ludicrously irrelevant in face of the great universal Reali-

[1] See the earlier letter of April 15, 1929.

ties. And then (a rather unexpected but logical outcome) the pettinesses of my Order and even of the Church affecting me but little, I find myself much more free to appreciate their marvellous treasure of religious experience and their unique power of divinisation; and I'm more at peace than ever within them, though at a different level—having had 'to give the Fire its share.'[1]

Intellectually, I have been so absorbed by geology that I've still not had time to draft a study, which has now more or less matured, on 'Spiritual Energy' (considered as a new department with which physics must be invested): yet again an extension of my views on the Noosphere which you know already. At a certain moment I had a hope of publishing a fairly substantial article on the Foundations of Evolution (written in 1926). The *Revue des Questions Scientifiques* (Louvain) had been badgering me for it. All was ready. Then the Malines diocesan censorship put in its veto at the last minute! However, to get its own back, the Review is going to quote *in extenso* a much shorter, but equally solid article which has been published *here* in a little review produced by the Apostolic Legation in Peking.[2] Also from Louvain they wrote to me (last July) that *Le Milieu Divin* was going to be printed. Since then, not a word.[3] Doubtless some flaw has been found there, too. I haven't seen Vialleton's book.[4] Always the same negative criticism and vague nominalism, I imagine. It's much better to build than to argue to no purpose (especially if the censors prevent

[1] The allusion is to Mlle Zanta's novel, *La part du feu*, Paris, Plon, 1927.

[2] Cf. above, the letter of April 15, 1929.

[3] On July 8, 1929, Père Charles wrote to Père Teilhard to say that *Le Milieu Divin* was on the point of going to press, and that 'all the censors are extremely favourable.' Cf. *Letters from a Traveller*, p. 159, and Claude Cuénot, *Teilhard de Chardin*, p. 118.

[4] Louis Vialleton, *L'origine des êtres vivants. L'illusion transformiste*, Plon, 1929.

you from answering). As regards this, the greater part of a skull has just been discovered near Peking in some big excavations in which I've been closely involved; it seems exactly to mark the transition between Pithecanthropus and Neanderthal Man. You're bound to hear of it through the newspapers and magazines. That'll make a big splash in the still waters of the Theologians.

I'm a bit worried about Marguerite these days. She is depressed by Cécile's crisis, and she seems less and less able to rise above the pain of the separation. It weighs on me all the more as I feel rather responsible for our very great friendship. . . .[1]

Yours ever—and don't forget me,
P. Teilhard, s.j.

Tientsin,
February 7, 1930

How can I thank you enough, my very dear friend, for your strong and affectionate letter of January 7 which reached me this evening! I read it with joy; and as usual, as when going down your stairs (invariably late) and dashing to the Porte Maillot, I drew from it a pure impression of gentle strength. Thank you, infinitely. Yes, Le Puy Mary is a happy memory and an excellent symbol. But, in reality too, I need your support very much, as you are aware; it isn't only you who need mine.

What can I tell you about myself and China? Nothing very new since my last letter. Half my time has been spent in Peking (where I had a very gay '*Christmas*' with American friends) and the other half in Tientsin. While I was in Peking, '*Sinanthropus*' took up a great deal of

[1] Four lines of the manuscript are omitted.

my time, as I was entrusted with the 'presentation' of it from the geological point of view.[1] In Tientsin I've found relative calm, and I've been profiting by it to write some twenty pages on a subject which I have been turning over in my mind for the last four years: 'The Phenomenon of Man.'[2] I feel that this last essay, short though it is, marks an appreciable advance on its predecessors. I have sent it on the off-chance to Louvain. But once again I am learning by experience how much we must seize opportunities, in life, in proportion as they are offered. As regards tranquillity, this winter has nothing in common with the winter of 1926–27, when I enjoyed such deep peace for the writing of *Le Milieu Divin*! Never again, I feel, shall I come on such an oasis. Since I've been working with the Geological Survey of Peking, my time in China is almost as fully taken up as at the Museum —while I miss, alas, the solid spiritual excitement of Paris.

As I wrote to Marguerite a few days ago, my plans for the immediate future are becoming clearer. After a shortish trip this spring and summer, I would like (if Lyons permits: I've written to ask) to spend the autumn (that's all! . . .) in Paris, and then come back here in January 1931 to join the Citroën Yellow Expedition on which I would be *the* geologist, representing the Geological Survey of China. I shall admit to you, dear friend, that in all these things (these journeys in China, I mean) I am proceeding more and more tenaciously, with perhaps an ever deeper sense of purpose, but with less and less sense of joy. . . . At the risk of saying the same thing over and over again, I can only tell you what I feel in this way: I have the impression that I have moved into a state of

[1] On the discovery of *Sinanthropus* at Choukoutien, in December 1929, cf. C. Cuénot, *op. cit.*, pp. 96–9.

[2] A further reference to the article which was to appear in *La Revue des Questions Scientifiques* the following November. See comment p. 82n.

'force', as if something had driven me out of myself and taken my place and was now pushing me onwards. And then, in these last days, while writing to Marguerite, I found another formula to express the calm that came to me this summer regarding so many things that used to irritate me, and that now I look on with 'gentleness'; it seems to me that, though still always reaching out to '*What is coming*,' but accepting that this New Thing can only be born of fidelity to *what is*, I now find myself 'beyond revolt.' The expression is rather paradoxical, but it conveys well what I feel, and by what intermediaries I have got there.

I'm delighted for your sake that *Sainte-Odile* has made her appearance. What are you doing now, if you have time to do anything? My best wishes to Donnay. Make him read and lend him anything you like. I still have no news of *Le Milieu Divin*, which supposedly went to the printers last summer. Another hold-up, no doubt. Thank you for letting me know of dear Vialleton's death[1]—he had a good heart, though his understanding was a bit limited. What is he thinking now? ... A terrifying mystery, the next world. And how prepare for it better than by passionately serving, for God and in God, this universe which takes us all back into itself, one after another.

Please remember me with affection to the little family. Fresh news soon.

Your friend,
P. Teilhard, s.j.[2]

[1] Louis Vialleton had just died, in January 1930.

[2] Two lines of post-script are omitted.

Tientsin,
April 3, 1930

Very dear friend,

Your fine long letter of March 6 reached me safely a few days ago; and as usual it brought me a message of gentle strength. I wonder if these lines will reach you before you leave for Spain? I hope so—so that you can take with you, on your splendid trip, the assurance that my faithful thoughts will follow you among the wonders that await you. Your eyes and your soul will be enriched among those glories of the past. But if you're exactly like me, it won't be possible for you to find true rest, or true satisfaction, in beauties among which it would be intolerable for us to live nowadays (because they were the product of a 'soul' that we left behind us long ago). The greatest pleasure that a Gothic cathedral gives me (though I find the building marvellous) is the 'triumphant' knowledge that our spirit has for ever escaped outside its arches! In the past, I would never have dared to write such a phrase (though it expresses what I already thought without daring to admit it to myself). But, now, I believe that we must shout the truth from the housetops. This is an effect of the invasion of myself by 'the Other,' which I have already mentioned: all 'complacency' about the Past (even the Christian past), or even about the Present, has become intolerable to me. And I believe that possession of minds and souls will be given to him who can best make known this Gospel (an authentic echo, as I see things, of Christ's): 'Forever forward.' '*No retreat.*' I found what you said about Bergson deeply moving. I pray for that admirable man and venerate him as a kind of saint. I've written to Auguste Valensin asking him to

try to see him, through and with Le Roy.[1] What's become of Le Roy, incidentally, and of his book on God ?[2]
I'm rather worried. Another condemnation would do
enormous harm to the current of thought that our friend
was beginning to canalise.

My own life is always the same. A lot of geological
work and not enough time for thought and composition.
I've been asked for (and I'd like to write it) a sort of exposition of Christianity for the use of Young China. It
would be called: 'The Place of Christianity in the Universe.'[3] I would have to show (a) how Religion corresponds to an essential and continually growing function
of universal evolution, and (b) how Christianity is in
fact the only form of religion currently viable (*in spite
of*, or rather, precisely *because of*, the part it gives to Personality and to some Revelation). I can see fairly clearly
what must be said. But when shall I get the time to write
it ? I'm just embarking on an endless period of travel and
unrest: a trip to Manchuria around April 20; then a possible trip to the Eastern Gobi with the Andrews Expedition; then, I hope, a brief return to Europe in the autumn
(with the joy of seeing you again!); then the Yellow Expedition. I advance ever more lost in the Force that leads
me on.

[1] In fact Père Auguste Valensin had been seeing Bergson since 1928.
After one of these early meetings he wrote: 'Great *reciprocal* sympathy;
very different from Blondel: less flow, but also less splash; sure, im-
peccable advance, without repetition' (quoted in *Auguste Valensin.
Textes et documents inédits*, Paris, Aubier, 1961, p. 206). See also pp. 296-
7 and pp. 307-8, for extracts of the 'homage' published in January,
1941, in *L'Éveil de Nice* and *La Croix* a few days after Bergson's death.
On meetings with Le Roy, cf. *ibid.*, p. 249.

[2] An allusion to the book Le Roy was writing on the problem of
God: *Le Problème de Dieu*. Cf. the letter of March 20, 1932.

[3] This 'exposition' seems never to have been written. But it became
the subject-matter of the lectures (now lost) given at Chadefaud in
November and December of that year: *Essai d'intégration de l'homme
dans l'univers*.

Always keep me in touch with what you are doing, writing, or thinking. You know full well how dear your support and sympathy are to me. There are lots of things to be said and distinctions to be made regarding friendship as compared with love. . . . But it would be better to analyse all that in your dear little 'den' than in dissertations by correspondence. We'll have that session in the autumn, I hope. In any case, a thousand wishes for the happiness of the two little fiancées.[1] Everything moves devilishly fast in your neighbouring flat!

More news soon.

Yours ever,
P. Teilhard, s.j.

The famous *Sinanthropus* skull is proving more and more to be a find of the first order—a solid fact that's going to be highly embarrassing to many out-of-date minds.

The National Geological Survey of China,
August 22, 1930

Very dear friend,

Just a few lines to thank you for your kind letter from Brittany. I know the mouth of the river Rance: it reminds me of August 1901, when I was a budding Jesuit and on my way to Jersey for the first time, driven out by those expulsions whose ultimate consequence was to send me to China, and to make your acquaintance—which is quite a lot.

I'm expecting to leave Peking on September 10, via Siberia, and to reach Paris towards September 25 (I shall let you know at once, though I don't suppose you'll be

[1] Marthe and Monique Gallichon, Mlle Zanta's nieces.

back before October). We'll have a great deal to talk
about. Physically, I don't feel so young; but I feel that
I 'see' better now than ever before—very simply, very
coldly, and very passionately, all at the same time! I
shall tell you my plans for inner construction, through
lack of plans for outward influence—regarding which
I'm always considerably cramped. However, Louvain
(*Revue des Questions Scientifiques*) is now very keen on a
short article on the 'Phenomenon of Man,'[1] an article
which I rather feared had made the editorial staff think
me a bit mad. It could lead the way to developments;
whereas *Le Milieu Divin* seems thoroughly dead and
buried. It should have been printed a year ago! But I'm
philosophical now, not exactly stoical, but deeply convinced of the 'inexistence' of human obstacles as against
the march of truth.

Yours,
P. Teilhard, s.j.

Peking,
March 20, 1932

Very dear friend,
I'm very cross with myself for not having answered
your kind cards of last summer and your excellent letter
of November 6 during this month that I've been back—
they all reached me safely. If I haven't written during
these months when I've been constantly on the move,
you know well that it isn't because my mind and heart
have not been with you.
I don't know what to say, after such a long silence,
except that I would love to spend a whole afternoon sitting beside you and talking about whatever came into

[1] Cf. above, p.100.

my head—countries, people, ideas, new experiences.
That will happen, I hope, next autumn. Meanwhile, I'd
like you to know that all in all I am very pleased that I
accompanied the Expedition;[1] the trip had few charms
(in the superficial sense of the word), and there were
annoyances throughout, but, apart from all that, there
was the overpowering interest of doubling my knowledge of Asia. And you know that this professional side
of things is one of the most substantial aspects of my
activity: for is not the passion to seek and to find one of
the most vital expressions of Religion and Mysticism?
You'll have heard from the newspapers of how this rather
flashy undertaking of the Expedition was brought to an
end by the sudden death of Haardt,[2] who succumbed
in Hongkong to a recurrence of the pneumonia that he
had contracted, I think, on arrival in Peking. It was a real
sadness to me that I couldn't be by his side at the end—
he was such a sincere and generous man and I know he
would have liked my support. For all sorts of reasons,
I was unable to accompany the Expedition into Indo-
China and the disaster happened when I was no longer
there.

Now that I have made a rather abrupt return to the
semi-religious life, the period (long though it was!) that
I spent in travelling already seems well in the past. Once
again I was able to observe how much the 'lay' milieu
is my 'natural' milieu. Yet I have found no difficulty in
returning to the minimum ecclesiastical framework in
which life has placed me. I don't take it 'seriously' enough
any longer for it to cause me deep suffering. And then I

[1] The 'Yellow Expedition' (May 1931-February 1932). Cf. *Letters
from a Traveller*, pp. 174-93, and Claude Cuénot, *op. cit.*, pp. 125-34.
Père Teilhard had been back in Peking since February 12.

[2] Georges-Marie Haardt, who organised the Yellow Expedition after
having directed the Black Expedition.

keep telling myself that if I were less deeply inserted within the Church, I would be less equipped for the work of setting her free.[1] Soon after my return, I made my eight-day retreat so as to get possession over my inner self again; and then I resumed my work in Peking—my presence there is becoming more and more wanted and needed by the Survey. Henceforth I can no more see myself making a final break with China than with Paris. I am not intending to make any but short trips before returning to France (before winter). I've had my fill; and then getting around is becoming harder and harder in this country.

Marguerite will have told you that, thanks to my absence and to a noble defence by my Order (which, I fear, was thinking more of its own reputation than of saving me), there seems no reason to think that I have anything to fear from any disagreeable backwash from the Le Roy affair. Like you, I am sorry that an excessive concern for clarity and honesty made him (Le Roy) provide a pretext in the first part of his *Problème de Dieu* for condemning three and a half books that to me seem beyond attack,[2] and for throwing suspicion on tendencies

[1] Père de Lubac's preface sheds light on the difficulties Père Teilhard ran up against and the nature of his reaction.

[2] The 'Le Roy affair' occurred when by a decree of the Holy Office, June 24, 1931 (*Acta Apostolicae Sedis*, 1931, p. 330), a number of his books were put on the Index: *L'exigence idéaliste et le fait de l'évolution* (1927), *Les origines humaines et l'évolution de l'intelligence* (1928), *Le Problème de Dieu* (1929), and the second volume of *La Pensée intuitive* (1930). In all, 'three and a half books.' Père Teilhard sees the cause of the step taken against Le Roy's other books as lying in the criticisms of the proofs of the existence of God contained in the first part of *Le Problème de Dieu*. He wrote to Père Valensin about the 'affair' on March 13 (hence a week before his letter to Mlle Zanta): 'I suppose it's the first half of "La Connaissance de Dieu" that has unleashed a wholesale condemnation; in three-quarters of the four volumes condemned, plus a half of the remaining volume, I can't see where criticism has anything serious to bite into—save, perhaps, taking exception to a ten-

and an outlook in which I see the dawn of a new Christianity. But I am determined, personally, to go ahead just as in the past. To begin with I'm going to try to make the minor adjustments to *Le Milieu Divin* that have been requested, with a view to eventual publication (?). Then, at the first possible opportunity, I propose to write something new on the fundamental metaphysical and religious question: 'What is the Multiple, and how can it be reduced to Unity?' (the eastern solution, and the western solution). Once again, how much would I give to be able to discuss all these things with you.

Here, as in France, there is a good deal of pessimism. I think we must resist this wave of apprehension about the great metamorphoses that are taking place. The only people who have a right to groan are those who have tied up their universe with disappearing forms, or who do not believe that the world has the power or the need to renew itself. Neither you nor I are in either category.

Very affectionately yours in Christo,
P. Teilhard, s.j.

The National Geological Survey of China,
June 24, 1934

Very dear friend,
When I came back from the depths of Szechwan five days ago, and found your Easter letter, it was like a

---

dency or *Weltanschauung* (but isn't that really just what has happened?). I know that Le Roy accompanied his recantation (which I haven't yet seen) with a letter in which he explained that his recantation "whose meaning he did not understand" signified only his desire to obey the Church. I would be surprised if this gesture made him look smaller—even in the eyes of the "Gentiles".'

sweet breeze. No need to tell you that for months I've been living with the *intention* of writing to you. And now, here we are!... Thank you for the photo. And thank you most of all for your friendship. And thank you for the calm and serenity that you irradiate by this friendship. What a precious and *rare* thing you are! and how I would love, after such a long time, to be able to recover my strength a little, near to you!

How can I possibly describe, in a letter, what point I've reached after over a year's absence?

Essentially there's nothing new as regards me, either in China, in Rome, or in Paris. Here, in spite of the un-expected death of Dr Black[1] (his disappearance is one of the greatest griefs of my life), our lines of research remain the same. We're still finding evidence of Sinanthropus at Choukoutien, and since Easter I've been constantly visiting the Yangtse valley—from Nanking as far as the lowest foothills of Tibet. There is nothing to indicate that my chances (and obligations) of work in China are on the decline; very much the reverse! I'm getting used to the idea of ending my days here, though of course I'm not abandoning my determination to remain in con-tact with Paris. But I'm not at all sure that I'll be able to put in an appearance in France this winter. Black's death involves me in still greater devotion to my post. And I can't provide any clear-cut reason to justify a journey to Europe. But nothing has been decided. I both want and fear those fleeting visits to Paris.

In Rome there has been some vague idea of inviting me to come and have a 'talk.' But I can't quite see how I could make an honourable peace. My friend, Père de

[1] On March 16 Dr Davidson Black, director of the Geological Survey, had died of a heart attack in his laboratory in Peking, 'between *Sinan-thropus* and the skull of the Upper Cave.' Cf. George B. Barbour, *In the Field with Teilhard de Chardin*, New York, Herder & Herder, 1965. Père Teilhard had worked with Black for over ten years.

Bonneville (provincial in Lyons) is the first to advise me against such a visit *ad limina*. So I'm not budging. It seems that there have been more complaints about me this winter. I only know of one (utterly absurd) concerning a purely technical report submitted to *L'Anthropologie*—it had no follow-up. But I've obviously a loaded dossier against me, and there are plenty of mines lurking in the waters where I sail.

I have relatively little news from Paris. But I note, from the few books that I receive (mainly from *Vie Intellectuelle* sources),[1] that some ideas, and even expressions, are gently making headway—to the extent of appearing from the great pen of Sertillanges.[2] That helps me to be patient. All the same I'd like to go and get a closer look at things, and give them a fresh impetus.

This is enough to show you that in my heart I haven't changed, except along the same lines. One consequence of this movement is that I am gradually finding myself more and more on the fringe of a lot of things. It's only thanks to the exotic life I'm leading that this drift doesn't develop into a break. What rather reassures me and saves me is that, if a whole wall of ecclesiastical concepts and conventions has definitively collapsed around me, I have never, on the other hand, felt nearer to what seem to me the deeper axes of Christianity: the future value of the world, the primacy of the Spirit and the Personality, divine Personality. I can see no way out, nor any strength for me, outside the (theoretical *and* practical) synthesis of passionate faith in the world and passionate faith in God.

---

[1] The well-known Dominican review (Tr.).

[2] In particular cf. *Dieu ou rien?* by A.-D. Sertillanges, Paris, Flammarion, 1933, vol. I, chap. 1 ('God and the world') and chap. 2 ('God and the origins of man'), pp. 9-149. As regards *Dieu ou rien?*, Père Teilhard wrote an important letter to Père Sertillanges, published in A. D. Sertillanges, *L'ame et l'univers*, Paris, Editions ouvrières, 1965, pp. 16-17.

Being fully human and Christian, one through the other. This leads to situations that appear paradoxical. But I am more and more determined to put my trust in Life, without letting anything surprise me. And then I feel that I haven't the least apprehension about anything that could happen to me, provided that it is 'in the service of the world.'

This winter I was able to do some writing again. First of all an essay that came out pretty well on *Christology and Evolution*,[1] in which I condensed into twenty pages the essence of almost all my papers of the last twenty years. And then a sketch, in a less finished form, on the *Evolution of Chastity*.[2] The first essay has been shown only to Auguste Valensin, de Lubac, Le Roy, Charles, Maréchal. So far only Valensin has given his opinion: he considers it one of my best Notes (!), which certainly doesn't mean that he approves of everything in it. The second piece is still in my drawer—because it runs the risk of being misunderstood. But it's an absolutely honest and disinterested attempt to get to the bottom of a question that seems to me terribly vital and terribly obscure. I have gathered together the most fundamental evidence that I've ever been able to find in face of questions and challenges that were anything but abstract, so as to build up 'the defence' and above all so as to define the value or essence 'of chastity.' We must have a talk about this. In last analysis, it is simply, but in its acutest form !, the problem of matter,—and of the spiritual power of matter. I've various other writings in view, notably a statement about 'My belief' for Mgr Bruno de Solages (Toulouse),

[1] *Christologie et évolution*, a typescript of 22 pages written in Tientsin, Christmas, 1933.

[2] *L'évolution de la chasteté*, typescript, 26 pages, written in Peking in February, 1934.

who circulates my papers widely[1]—and also a 'Sacrament of the world'[2] in which I would like to take up, on a much deeper level, my 'Mass on the world.' But when shall I find the time? . . .

So, here you have three large pages in which I've spoken only of myself; but by confessing to you—which is surely the best gift of oneself. Write to me often. I shall reply more promptly in future. And then, may God preserve your beneficial serenity, and increase in us both the taste for Being.

Yours,
P. Teilhard, s.j.

Please remember me to our common friends whom I have met in your little home in Neuilly: Donnay, Garric, 'Salinas,'[3] etc. I forget no one.[4]

S.S. Tjinagara (off Shanghai),
January 26, 1936

Dearest friend,

Before all the hurly-burly that lies ahead on my arrival in China tomorrow, I want to send you some news with my delayed New Year wishes, so as to keep up the beneficial contact between us. I owe you *so much*, dear friend, and it is such sweetness, both for my mind and heart,

[1] This was *Comment je crois*, 40 pages of typescript written in Peking and dated October 28, 1934. Mgr de Solages was to quote it at length in *Le Livre de l'espérance*, Paris, Spes, 1954, pp. 58-60. It is now published in *Le coeur de la Matière*, Vol. 10 of Pierre Teilhard de Chardin's works (1966).

[2] *Le Sacrement du Monde* never got further than the planning stage.

[3] Madame Darcanne, one of the first woman house-surgeons in France. She was also the author of a life of Mlle Zanta. Cf. above, p. 24.

[4] Five lines of post-script are omitted.

to find you there again on each return to Europe—always wise, steadfast and loving. Oh if only women were all like you. . . . But then the conquest of Fire (a nice title for a novel, don't you think?) would be too easy.

Outwardly, since I left France last September, my life has been nothing but high adventure. As soon as I got to India I went up to Kashmir—an incredible basket of greenery, reddening under the first touches of autumn, between the snowy mountain chains of the Pir Panjal (higher than Mont Blanc) and the soaring Himalayas. Then I spent two months in the deserts or semi-deserts of the Punjab and the middle Indus. Finally, to end up, we took our camp beds up into the enchanting Narbada valley (central India), in a setting of jungle, monkeys and parrots. During all that time we never stopped collecting an abundance of new things. After that I went from Calcutta down to Java where another friend (young von Koenigswald, another delightful German)[1] showed me further extraordinary new discoveries in prehistory, in a setting of volcanoes and palm trees. Finally, eleven days ago, I boarded the Dutch steamer I am now travelling on at Batavia. And slowly, against the monsoon and under an ever-increasingly cold grey sky (there was snow this morning on the Fukien mountains), we are approaching the mud of the Yangtse—which, now, I can't wait to see. There's so much awaiting me in Peking in the way of people and things! How shall I find my Geological Survey after the latest Japanese push? But in spite of this pang of uneasiness, which grows as we draw nearer, I'm basically pleased that I didn't miss out on an experience (the Indian journey) that I viewed at first with some apprehension. From the technical point of view, this last autumn will have considerably broadened and raised

[1] 'The young and brilliant Koenigswald' (*Letters from a Traveller*, p. 221), a German scientist, had invited Père Teilhard to Java.
L.L.Z.

my scientific platform. Though I have more and more definitively lost my illusions as to the benefit to mankind at this stage of persistently discovering yet more about the past, yet the fact remains that I need a platform so as to get a hearing on more important points. So all goes well. Once again I did right to follow to the end the thread that life held out to me.

What increasingly dominates my interest and my inner preoccupations, as you already know, is the effort to establish within myself, and to diffuse around me, a new religion (let's call it an improved Christianity, if you like) whose personal God is no longer the great 'neolithic' landowner of times gone by, but the Soul of the world— as demanded by the cultural and religious stage we have now reached. Above all since I left Calcutta, and during the twenty or so days of solitude on board, I've been thinking a lot—and praying too. My road ahead seems clearly marked out; it is a matter not of superimposing Christ on the world, but of 'panchristising' the universe. The delicate point (and I touched on part of this in *Christology and Evolution*) is that, if you follow this path, you are led not only to widening your views, but to turning your perspectives upside down; evil (no longer punishment for a fault, but 'sign and effect' of progress) and matter (no longer a guilty and lower element, but 'the stuff of the Spirit') assume a meaning diametrically opposed to the meaning *customarily* viewed as Christian. Christ emerges from the transformation incredibly enlarged (at least that is my opinion—and all the uneasy contemporaries with whom I have spoken about it think like me). But is this Christ really the Christ of the Gospel? And if not, on what henceforward do we base what we are trying to build? I don't know whether, among the many of my colleagues who are in front of me or behind me on the road I am travelling, there are any (or even a single one! . . . that seems incredible) who realise the importance of the step that all are taking. But I'm beginning to see it very clearly. One thing reassures me: it is that, in me, the increase of light goes hand in hand with love, and with renouncement of myself in the Greater than me. This could not deceive. Thus in an obscure way I fall back on the feelings that Being is infinitely richer and more able to bring renewal than our logic. As all forms of movement, the paradox of the religious change now in progress will resolve itself by its very movement. 'Solvitur eundo.'

Under the impulse of preoccupations such as these, I am feeling my way towards the writing of another essay, which will group together, I think, the best of my latest conquests: *The Personal Universe* or, better, (A Sketch for) *A Personal Universe*.[1] In it I would like to analyse what happens to the world once one agrees to make a place in it for the 'personal' (which is an unquestionable fact—and even the foundation—of experience). Step by step everything is transformed, morality merges with physics, individuality is extended into universality, matter becomes the structure of Spirit. And we arrive at a picture very close to the neo-Christianity about which I was speaking earlier on. I don't want to hurry myself about writing this. But I can feel the ideas clarifying themselves and becoming more organised.

Another point of view: in the last months I've had the opportunity of developing my knowledge of the peoples of Asia. These new experiences have only reinforced my conviction that nothing could be more dangerous for 'humanitarians' (to whose company I belong) than to

---

[1] Three months later, in Peking on May 4, he wrote his *Esquisse d'un univers personnel*, published in *L'Énergie humaine*, vol. 6 of Pierre Teilhard de Chardin's Works (1962), pp. 67-114.

shut their eyes to the fact of the complexity (or hetero-
geneity) of the human mass. As I explained in a (private)
letter to Maurice Brillant, about a pro-Abyssinian mani-
festo that I was asked (happily, too late) to sign, the
philosophical or 'supernatural' unity of human nature
has *nothing* to do with the equality of races in what concerns their physical capacities to contribute to the building
of the world. Now it is the *latter* point, and not the *former*,
that we are dealing with in the Abyssinian and Chinese
questions. Under the false invocation of 'war of expan-
sion' (immoral in itself: 'the right of the strongest') I
think in some confused way we are to understand 'war
of construction' (that is to say the right of the earth to
organise itself by reducing, even by *force*, the refractory
and backwards elements). In this sense, in *last analysis*,
I am with Mussolini against the liberals of the left and
the missiologists. Mussolini seems to me to be most
wrong when he uses force in a cowardly and gratuitous
way (when other factors could have been brought into
play), and does so at the risk of disturbing the ideas and
agreements painfully built up by the Western bloc. I
would like to write an article about this. But I would
never find anyone to approve, nor any review to publish
it.[1] And yet the objective fact seems to me this: (1) no
international morality is possible without previous accep-
tance that there is an earth to be constructed which trans-
cends states; (2) and once this construction has been agreed
to, everything must give way; and, as not all ethnic
groups have the same value, they must be dominated

[1] Père Teilhard took up these ideas again in *Sauvons l'humanité*,
Peking, November 11, 1936 (34 pp. of typescript). A shortened version
of the text appeared in *Études*, October 20, 1937, vol. 233, pp. 145-65,
with the title *La Crise présente: réflexions d'un naturaliste*. The original
text is published in P. Teilhard de Chardin, *Science et Christ*, Paris,
Seuil, 1965, pp. 167-91; Eng. trs. *Science and Christ*, London, Collins,
1968 pp. 128-50

which does not mean they must be despised—quite the reverse).*

To return to my experiences, India did not seem to me to have preserved much more creative power than China or Japan. And its present-day religion is as good a warning as any for a Church which could run the risk of letting itself be dominated by ritual and all forms—however well disguised—of superstition. Sometimes I've trembled in recognising ourselves 'in them.'

Goodbye, dear friend. As you see, I ramble on as if I were in your flat. But it's much less soothing.

'*God bless you.*'
P. Teilhard, s.j.

* In other words, *at one and the same time* there should be official recognition of:

1. The $\left\{\begin{array}{l}\text{priority}\\\text{primacy}\end{array}\right\}$ of the earth over nations;
2. The inequality of peoples and races.

Now the *second* point is currently reviled by Communism . . . and the Church, and the *first* point is similarly reviled by the Fascist systems (and, of course, by less gifted peoples!)

So everyone at once will fall on the man who tells the truth. And yet, *if* it's the truth. . . .

Paris,
November 12, 1938

Dear friend,

Thank you for your kind letter. Marguerite had already told me, and anyway I had a shrewd suspicion that your life weighed heavily on you. We shall help each other to make spirit emerge from the weight of matter. . . .

It's impossible for me to get free in the next few days. But I want to see you very much. I believe we shall be meeting at Marguerite's next Saturday. And then I expect to be able to fix a meeting with you in your little nest at Neuilly, which brings so many tender thoughts to my mind.

Affectionately,
P. Teilhard, s.j.

I'll be taking to Marguerite's the number of *Recherches*,[1] if I don't put it in the post earlier.

Paris
November 21, 1938

Ever dear friend,

I was so very distressed to hear that you still couldn't move last Saturday, and so distressed, too, at having to leave for Lyons tomorrow. Heaven bless or confound the Superior who wants to see me instead of writing to me, and about things that will amount to nothing! . . . I'll be back on Friday evening but will be taken up on Saturday and Sunday (a meeting that I cannot miss). Suggest some possible times during the following week. I want to see you so much.

May Our Lord keep you in his *deep* peace and joy.

Affectionately always,
P. Teilhard, s.j.

---

[1] i.e. the issue of *Recherches de science religieuse* which contained Père Jules Lebreton's study: *Sainte Monique et saint Augustin: la vision d'Ostie*, vol. 28 (1938) pp. 457-72. Mlle Zanta was writing *Sainte Monique et son fils: la mère chrétienne*, Paris, Plon, 1941.

Paris,
February 11, 1939

Dear friend,

Something has cropped up at the last moment which would make it difficult for me to come on Sunday 12. Would you forgive me if I came the following Sunday, the 19? My very dear friend Bégouën[1] is unexpectedly leaving for Africa on Monday (for three or four months!) and the only day I can see him before his long absence is the 12th. You understand that if February 19, at 4, suits you, don't bother to answer.

Affectionately,
P. Teilhard, s.j.

I'm so pleased, so *happy*, to know you're in good form. I'll try to bring you *La Vision d'Ostie*.[2] Père Lebreton spoke to me very highly of it.

Tuesday[3]

Dear Mademoiselle and friend,

I too long to see you again, for obviously our Sunday gathering, which I found *very good*, left some loose ends. Unfortunately I'm not free on Sunday. If I don't go to England, I'll let you know. Anyway, till the first possible moment!

I've been giving more thought to the immortality of the soul. Plainly that immortality derives from the fact that in us the monad (that is to say the world) has gathered

[1] Comte Max Bégouën.
[2] Père Paul Henry's *La Vision d'Ostie*, Paris, 1938. Cf. above, p.118 n.
[3] This letter has no date in the original manuscript.

itself into a definitive centre. But by what sign are we to recognise that this organic phenomenon has taken place? . . . Doubtless by our power of reflection and idealisation. But—and I become more and more convinced of it—there is another sign. If the person did not persist, our inner and most priceless work would become vain, we would no longer have sufficient reason for acting, and then the perspective of death would be intolerable. The double burden 1. of action to be carried out, and 2. of death to be faced, can only be admitted for a conscious (reflective) being, if the soul is immortal. In this way *immortality* and *reflection are necessarily associated*, not only by metaphysical or physical necessity, but by *moral necessity*. A universe in which the second were to appear without the first would not only be an absurd world but, what is almost more serious, a hateful world.

Yours affectionately,

P. Teilhard, s.j.[1]

---

[1] Mlle Zanta was to die on June 14, 1942. Père A.-D. Sertillanges gave her extreme unction and wrote an obituary article about her in *Les Voix françaises*, July 17, 1942.

Index

Léontine Zanta was brilliant, delightful, and in her day famous. She was the first Frenchwoman to become a doctor of philosophy, an inspired teacher and the centre of a lively group of writers and thinkers. She was also a dedicated friend, who, until the end of her life (she died in 1942), kept up an active correspondence with innumerable people: guiding, advising, questioning, and discussing her own activities and development.

She first met Père Teilhard de Chardin through his cousin Marguerite Teilhard-Chambon (to whom he addressed the letters published in *The Making of a Mind*), and there began a friendship of profound value to them both. Each was able to encourage, sustain and test out the thought of the other. Mademoiselle Zanta's letters to Teilhard in China kept him in touch with Paris, and with her he was able to discuss freely his ideas, anxieties, joys, as well as acting as spiritual guide. The letters in this collection cover the period 1923 to 1939, and are almost all written from China. They reveal many shared concerns, a deep mutual respect, and the letters concerning Teilhard's spiritual crisis with the Jesuits are intensely interesting.

Of the French edition of these letters, *The Times Literary Supplement* said: 'They give in little more than an hundred pages, a clear impression of the man, his vision and his mission.'